John XXIII and the City of Man

by PETER RIGA

N / P

THE NEWMAN PRESS

Westminster, Maryland

1 9 6 6

Nihil Obstat: Rev. Thomas J. McDonagh, C.S.C. *Censor Deputatus*
Imprimatur: Most Rev. Leo A. Pursley, D.D. *Bishop of Fort Wayne–
South Bend* January 15, 1966

The *nihil obstat* and *imprimatur* are official declarations that a book
or pamphlet is free of doctrinal and moral error. No implication is
contained therein that those who have granted the *nihil obstat* and
imprimatur agree with the opinions expressed therein.

The cease of majesty
Dies not alone, but like a gulf doth draw
What's near it with it; it is a massy wheel,
Fix'd on the summit of the highest mount,
To whose huge spokes ten thousand lesser things
Are mortised and adjoin'd; which, when it falls,
Each small annexment, petty consequence,
Attends the boisterous ruin.

Hamlet, III:3

Contents

Introduction ix

I   Some Basic Concepts of the Encyclical . . . 1

II Intermediate Groups and Unions 24

III Private Property 64

IV Agriculture 117

V   Economically Underdeveloped Nations . . . 142

VI The Spiritual and Temporal Task 192

Index I 232

Index II 236

Index III 238

Introduction

CHRISTIANITY has long been infected with a type of Gnostic Manichaeanism which considers the material world and the tasks within it unworthy of serious consideration by the Christian—if not evil. This Crypto-Gnosticism is not dead. In Christian circles there is a constant temptation to make little of human activities and temporal realities. All dualist doctrines which consider matter the work of an evil principle yield to this temptation.

Pope John XXIII confronts this error directly in his challenging encyclical *Mater et Magistra*. He emphatically declares that the material universe and the material labor of mankind are willed by God. Furthermore, this world which we see and touch has been re-created by the Incarnation of the Son of God. By reason of his nature, man stands on the horizon between matter and spirit. In the beautiful words of St. Hilary, "he is the bond of friendship uniting and glorifying all creation." Consequently, Christian man alone is capable of giving a human meaning to the material universe. The Pope emphasizes that this is the Christian vocation of the layman in the world: to establish the kingdom of Christ in the modern world.

As Pope John sees it in *Mater et Magistra,* the human community ought to be—or at least Christians ought to strive to make it—an imperfect but real reflection of the kingdom of heaven, where justice, peace, love, and freedom are perfect. The task is awesome in its extent and possibilities. Any attempt to avoid this responsibility will result in further alienating modern man from the living voice of the Gospel. Implementation of the teachings of *Mater et Magistra* will make the Church the strongest moral leader on earth. Failure to do so will make her a needless scandal to modern man, who longs for such leadership in a chaotic world.

✽

The encyclical *Mater et Magistra* is built on a foundation composed of four main themes. The first is a short historical resumé of the social teachings of the Church from Leo XIII (*Rerum Novarum*) up to and including the well-known radio message of Pius XII in 1941. From this, Pope John proceeds to enumerate the many and profound changes which have taken place on the economic and social plane since 1941. These transformations have occurred on a national and, above all, on an international plane (par. 1–49). Now, he concludes, is an opportune time to speak in a new encyclical (par. 50), in order to keep the social thought of the Church in step with the needs of the times. The Catholic must continuously study and make reference to this social teaching if he is to be guided by the true moral principles underlying human activities in the social and economic order; and the Church, in the person of the Soverign Pontiff, under the inspiration of the Holy Spirit, must make relevant the mind of Christ on the ever-changing social and economic situation of man. Without this Christian understanding, the Catholic is left impotent in his judgment of the modern situation which directs and controls the lives of men. The Pope makes this crystal clear when he says:

50. Therefore, We feel it Our duty to keep ablaze the torch first lit by Our great predecessors. We exhort all, therefore, to draw from it inspiration and direction in the search for a solution to the social question adapted to our times.

For this reason, on the occasion of the solemn commemoration of the Leonine encyclical, We are happy to have the opportunity to confirm and make more specific points of doctrine already treated by Our predecessors and, at the same time, to make clear the mind of the Church with respect to new and urgent problems of the day.

The second section of the encyclical also sheds new light on some of the older problems discussed in previous pontifical statements. It comprises five basic questions or categories which Pope John treats in separate paragraphs:

1) The increasing necessity of state intervention in social and economic matters. This was brought out in previous pontifical social thought but has now assumed even wider dimensions (par. 51–58).

2) The very important notion of "socialization," which stands as one of the focal points of modern life and, therefore, of Pope John's encyclical (par. 59–67).

3) The remuneration of work, which has also taken on new aspects with the worker's increased participation in industry (par. 68–81).

4) The demands of justice in the productive structure of the economy. This is an extention and development of the section on the remuneration of work (par. 82–103).

5) The concept of private property as extended in today's ever-expanding social and economic situation (par. 104–121).

The third section of the encyclical is an attempt to balance the various tensions in the social and economic sectors of society. Many types of disequilibrium are evident today in many sectors of the economy, and a just balance must be achieved between them: between rural and urban development (par. 123–149); between economically developed and underdeveloped nations (par. 150–184); and finally between population growth and the means of sustenance (par. 185–211). This leads the Pope to discuss these questions from an international and universalist point of view which is one of the salient features of his encyclical.

The fourth and final section of the letter (par. 212–265) has to do with the vocation of man both in its terrestrial and its specifically religious dimensions. Both of these aspects go to make up the fundamental Christian vocation of man. To construct a society here below without recognition of God and of properly spiritual values is to distort man himself; but at the same time, the Christian vocation demands that man become engaged in temporal tasks here below. Herein lies the fundamental importance of the Church's social teachings, which take the totality of man, body and soul, into consideration. He is, in the words of the Pope, "intrinsically social" by nature, both in his natural and supernatural vocation. Only in this way can the full dignity of the human person be safeguarded. Thus, the Pope concludes that this social teaching of the Church is not an afterthought attached to Christian doctrine. It is part and parcel of Christian teaching; as such, it must be studied and, above all, put into effective action. Christians must engage themselves in the tasks of this world, cooperating with each other and with all men of good will. Christian perfection is inconceivable without temporal engagement in the tasks, problems, and agonies of modern man. Always conscious of the fact that they are members of the Mystical Body of Christ, Catholics must be all the more conscious of justice in the world. They must strive to make this world a better place to live, a realm of justice and a domain worthy of the sacred being who is man. This is what the Pope calls "socialization," the divine-human vocation of the layman. Therefore the Pope says in par. 259:

> Hence, when Christians put themselves to work —even if it be in a task of a temporal nature—in conscious union with the divine Redeemer, every effort becomes a continuation of the effort of Jesus Christ and is penetrated with redemptive power: *He who abides in me, and I in him, he bears much fruit.* It thus becomes a more exalted and more noble labor, one which contributes to a man's personal spiritual perfection, helps to reach out and impart to others on all sides the fruits of Christian redemption. It further follows that the Christian message leavens, as it were, with the ferment of the Gospel the civilization in which one lives and works.

✤

The following chapters are an attempt to understand the mind of Pope John XXIII on these vital issues confronting the Church and modern man. We are convinced that without this guidance of the Pope, any *aggiornamento* of the Church is impossible.

PETER RIGA

Notre Dame University

CHAPTER ONE

Some Basic Concepts of the Encyclical

I

WITHIN THE CONTEXT of any papal encyclical there are several kinds of instruction, and each is applied with a different degree of emphasis. Thus one may find suggestions, directives, partial solutions, principles of social justice and philosophy, observations, counsels, and wishes. To weigh the relative worth of any of these particular pieces of instruction, it is first necessary to examine the total text of the encyclical.

Mater et Magistra is no exception. In fact, its great length (over 25,000 words) and the many fields of social philosophy and economics covered in it make an examination of the total text of the letter especially necessary. While each part must be closely studied—for no part of an encyclical is to be lightly taken—the general spirit and orientation of *Mater et Magistra* give it a tonality which will have its effect on the interpretation of its particular parts. *Mater et Magistra* is a complex document, dealing with a multitude of different social and economic topics. Pope John's judgment on each of these topics has many nuances. The reader must be careful not to confuse simple directives or suggestions with solemn principles of social justice which are also developed in the encyclical. Distinctions, emphases, and specific uses of terms in the context are all part of this close examination of the text; but above all, the unmistakable unity and spirit of the letter must guide interpretation.

Mater et Magistra is essentially pastoral in nature and orientated to positive action. "Good Pope John" often emphasizes that his children are not to lose time arguing over this or that point, or the authority of this or that statement.

> 238. In the application of this doctrine, however, there can sometimes arise—even among sincere Catholics—differences of opinion. When this happens, they should be alert to preserve and give evidence of their mutual esteem and respect. At the same time, they should strive to find points of agreement for efficacious and suitable action. They should take special care, moreover, not to exhaust themselves in interminable discussions and, under pretext of seeking the better or the best, fail meanwhile to do the good that is possible and is thus obligatory.

The tone of the encyclical is personalistic, human, and, above all, optimistic in its consideration of the future; furthermore, it is surprisingly free from condemnations and negativism. This tone coincides with the positive and optimistic pastoral concern of John XXIII. Only once does he directly mention Communism in negative terms (par. 34), and then he is explaining the social thought of Pius XI. That Pope John refrained from such condemnation came as a shock to many Catholics all over the world, who looked for another verbal blast against the Communist and Marxist systems.[1] But he was not satisfied to issue condemnations

---

[1] This same attitude was adopted by Vatican II in Schema XIII.

and did little of this. His main concern was to give a positive program which could be implemented by Catholics and all men of good will in helping modern man all over the world. Pope John was open, receptive, and sympathetic to modern society. Nowhere does one encounter the nostalgia for outdated structures or the ecclesiaticalism so characteristic of Catholics in the past. His attitude will probably prevail in history. Condemnations have never produced much fruit. The error must be known, but, more importantly, something must be done to alleviate the problem. Condemnations of Communism abound; programs for the development of world resources against disease, hunger, and human want are very few. In presenting these programs, the Pope sought to unite mankind in a worthy endeavor; and the search for that which unites is much more useful and important than concentration on that which divides and separates.

Other critics contend that *Mater et Magistra* has brought few or no new definitions and additions to the doctrines of Catholic social thought. This kind of criticism is erroneous and is born of hasty and imprecise reading. *Mater et Magistra* contains few new principles of social philosophy or natural law that touch on various aspects on social and economic justice, since the corpus of Catholic social thought from Leo XIII to Pius XII had already developed this aspect of the matter in full detail. In the first section of *Mater et Magistra* Pope John summarizes the social thought of his predecessors, but refrains from adding new principles because it was not necessary for his purpose. What he thought paramount was to apply the principles of his predecessors to the economic and social conditions which changed rapidly and turbulently from 1941 to 1961.

Despite Pope John's reluctance to enunciate new principles of social thought, the encyclical does give a rich social theology which unites the spiritual and temporal aspects of the Christian vocation here below. For the first time in a pontifical document, spirituality, temporality, and the apostolate are united in a total theological system. This unification is extremely important. In recent decades the position of the layman in the Church, the dialogue of the Church with the modern world, and a theology of terrestrial realities have been carefully examined and developed in theological and apostolic circles. In *Mater et Magistra* the Pope picked up these individual threads and wove them into a theological synthesis. He himself said that the letter was "a rich essay of moral-pastoral doctrine";[1] a letter which was and is in total conformity with the Gospel teachings of charity and justice.[2] In other words, he presupposes that the Catholic has already read, absorbed, and put into practice the directives and teachings of his predecessors in matters of social thought. In the present letter, the Pope did two things: he applied these principles to new situations which have arisen in the last twenty years or so, and he attempted to give a theological-pastoral synthesis which could be the practical basis for action in the modern world.

The pastoral concern of Pope John is evident throughout the letter. The tone of the letter is human and down to earth. It is an "*aggiornamento*" of Catholic thought to meet modern problems and difficulties. In colloquial English, the Pope wants us "to get with it." In paragraphs 234 through 238, he stresses that action is an essential element in the development of Catholic social thought. In other words, the Pope emphasizes that the

[1] *Osservatore Romano*, 12 June, 1962, p. 3.
[2] *Ibid.*

Christian is not only educated *for* action but *by* action. Christian education is no longer enough: it must be supplemented by concrete action on the firing line. The Catholic is called upon—in fact, is obliged—to become directly engaged in the social and economic activities of the modern world. Christian education is certainly necessary, but it must not be allowed to go unsupported by concrete action. This is the first time that any pontifical document has ever brought out this interaction and dependency so clearly.

The necessity for Christian education has been universally recognized in Catholic circles. What has not been so evident in Catholic thought is the necessity for concrete involvement in the social concerns of the modern world. The Pope made this bridge clearly and logically, giving full meaning to the motto "See, judge, act." This fusion of education and action fits in with Pope John's desire to give his flock a pastoral letter, a letter directed to concrete action, not to academic disputes. Such a letter will shock only those Catholics who have pictured the Church as an ivory tower, or, in Karl Marx's well-known phrase, as the opium of the people. The Pope shuns this misconception of the Church's mission and strives to make Christianity relevant to the problems of modern man.

As Pope John said so often, Christian social thought is a reflection of the Gospel and of the universal charity which teaches men that they are brothers. It is not and cannot be a partisan political or social view, though many Catholics would have it so. It is the continuation of the living voice of the Gospels applied to the affairs of the modern era. It is an integral part of the Christian conception of life (par. 222) and cannot be separated from the true Christian life without eviscerating the very notion of Christianity. It only becomes relevant when it sheds some light on the agonizing problems of modern man. This vital view of the Church's social teachings is at the center of *Mater et Magistra*, and with the authoritative voice and light of Christ Himself, the Pope urges Catholics to action in the world. To do otherwise is to fail in the Church's mission to be the light of the world, to be truly "Mother" as well as "Teacher" of the nations. Devoid of this teaching authority and failing to confront the real problems of real men in a real world, Christianity would be reduced to a pitiable irrelevance, a propagator of the *status quo*, and an inconsequential pietism.

II

To summarize, then, the work of John XXIII's predecessors laid a firm foundation of basic principles for Catholic social thought and action. The principle of subsidiarity, the right to organize, the right of private property and its corresponding social responsibility, the right and duty of state intervention, the desirability of social security, free initiative on the part of citizens, and other central concepts were fully presented and justified in Catholic social thought from the time of Leo XIII to that of Pius XII. John XXIII had this corpus to work with, and there was no need for him to reiterate it in detail. When this body of thought is treated in *Mater et Magistra*, it is applied to new situations and in a variety of ways which could not have been known to his predecessors simply because technology and the economic order have changed.

The intervention of the state in the economy is a good example of this change. Pope John points out what Leo XIII had said before him: because of the vastness, power, and complexity of the modern economy, the state has a positive right to intervene authoritatively to insure justice in all sectors of economic affairs. Repeating Leo XIII, he says:

> 20. The state, whose very reason for existence is the realization of the common good in the temporal order, cannot keep aloof from the economy. It should be present to promote in a suitable manner the production of a sufficient supply of material goods, *the use of which is necessary for the practice of virtue*, and to watch over the rights of all citizens, especially of the weaker among them, such as workers, women and children. It has also the inflexible duty of contributing actively to the betterment of the workers' standard of living.

The novelty of Pope John's teaching is that this principle is further extended. If the state had the right to intervene in economic and social matters in 1891, when society was not as complicated and developed as it is today, this right must apply with greater force now. State influence and intervention must necessarily be more extended today because the economy on a national and an international scale has become more vast and complicated.

In his discussion, the Pope maintains a balanced position between two extremes: those who would deny, as much as possible, any state regulatory activity in the economy, considering its necessity a lesser of two evils; and those who would permit the government to regulate or control the whole economic process by various types of socialism. For Pope John, intervention by the state is not an evil; rather, the state has a positive moral duty to maintain distributive justice in any given society and economy. State intervention, however, must not destroy the private initiative of the citizens; it must promote and safeguard it. This delicate balance is what the Popes have called the principle of subsidiarity: that is, the state helps or takes over for private groups and individuals only when they cannot do it themselves. Pope John reasons as follows:

> 51. At the outset it should be affirmed that in economic affairs first place is to be given to the private initiative of individual men who, either working by themselves, or with others in one fashion or another, pursue their common interests.
>
> .   .   .   .
>
> 53. This intervention of public authorities that encourages, stimulates, regulates, supplements, and complements, is based on the *principle* of *subsidiarity* as set forth by Pius XI in his Encyclical *Quadragesimo Anno:* "It is a fundamental principle of social philosophy, fixed and unchangeable, that one should not withdraw from individuals and commit to the community what they can accomplish by their own enterprise and industry. So, too, it is an injustice and at the same time a grave evil and a disturbance of right order, to transfer to the larger and higher collectivity functions which can be performed and provided for by lesser and subordinate bodies. Inasmuch as every social activity should, by its very nature, prove a help to members of the body social, it should never destroy or absorb them."

Thus the state's whole reason for existence is to be of service to the human person, promoting his progress and dignity. From the very beginning, the personalistic tone of this letter is evident. The state exists for the person, not the person for the state; the state intervenes in the social order to promote and safeguard human values, not to suppress them.

Ultimately, state intervention has a profound human meaning which was also brought out in *Pacem in terris* (par. 65–66). Each human person has a natural right to develop his talents, and he must do this of his own free will. In *Quadragesimo Anno*, Pope Pius XI capsulized this concept in the principle of subsidiarity: a society may not appropriate to itself the initiative which can be assumed by the individual. The foundation of this principle lies in the irreplaceable value of a person's free initiative in directing his destiny. Since each person must fulfill his own destiny through his own genius, he must be able to take advantage of all the means necessary to develop it. The function of the public authority is simply to create favorable conditions for this development.

The Pope also brings out the social reason that underpins the principle of subsidiarity: the riches and fruitfulness of society come from the diversity of its members, and this diversity is obviously related to the way in which each person develops his individual talents. The fullest exercise of human rights occurs when the individual's will keeps pace with his ability, and when his ability is confined by nothing but its own limitations. As this diversity is allowed to develop, society is enriched. That form of society then, which permits and encourages each of its members to perfect his potential, perfects itself, and by that very fact it becomes more personalistic in its conception of man. The Pope seems never to tire of drawing our attention to this personalism which must be evinced by any just social order.[3]

116. The doctrine that has been set forth above obviously does not prohibit the state and other public agencies from lawfully possessing produc-

[3] See par. 21, 23, 55, 61, 75, 106, 112, 114, 125, 144, 152, 160, 211, 213, 221–222, 258–259, etc.

*tive goods, particularly when they carry with them
an opportunity for domination that is so great that
it cannot be left in the hands of private individuals
without injury to the community at large.*

117. It seems characteristic of our times to vest
more and more ownership of goods in the state and
in other public bodies. This is partially explained
by the fact that the common good requires public
authorities to exercise ever greater responsibilities.
However, in this matter, the *principle of subsidiarity,* already mentioned above, is to be strictly
observed. For it is lawful for states and public
corporations to expand their domain of ownership
only when manifest and genuine requirements of
the common good so require, and then with safeguards, lest the possession of private citizens be
diminished beyond measure, or, what is worse,
destroyed.

In Western societies, this state power could encourage private initiative by such things as government
planning for all sectors of the economy, tax cuts in boom
periods as well as during recessions, insurance programs
for banks and other credit agencies, and, from a more
negative point of view, action against monopolies in
restraint of free trade. This latter action is an important
function of government because it protects small business and other types of free and private organization
which the Pope calls "intermediate bodies." As the Pope
says, "We consider it necessary that the intermediate
groups and numerous social enterprises through which
socialization tends to express itself should enjoy an
effective autonomy" (par. 65–66; see also par. 37 and
152).

Governments, notes the Pope, have gained immense

knowledge about depressions and "slump" periods. Their experiences in the past, especially during the 1930's, have shown them how to counter slumps: with easy money, tax cuts, easy credit, stepped-up spending, international cooperation on trade, and other measures. In the United States, there are legal safeguards against depressions through the Employment Act of 1946.

In underdeveloped countries, intervention by the state will obviously be greater than in those countries which are more highly developed economically. In order that each sector of the economy—agriculture, industry, and services—may develop in a balanced relationship to every other sector, the Pope gives his full approval to government planning and regulation of the economy (par. 151). Yet, this is but a temporary measure; and as soon as possible, or as soon as the common good permits it, private citizens and "intermediary bodies" ought to be allowed to take over (par. 152). The ideal situation is that public and private elements of the country work together for the common good. A balance must be maintained between the two, for a destruction of one by the other is immoral and contrary to the common good. When either of the two gains the ascendancy, an absolutist social system develops which is always harmful to the total well-being of society. In other words, society is to be seen as a total body which is kept balanced by the mutual cooperation of private and public enterprise.

57. Experience, in fact, shows that where the personal initiative of individuals is lacking, political tyranny appears. Moreover, stagnation occurs in a number of areas of the economy, and shortages are felt in a wide variety of consumer goods and services of a kind designed not only to meet mate-

rial wants, but more particularly to satisfy needs of the spirit, and which thus call into play in a special manner the creative talents of individuals.

58. Where the state fails to act in economic affairs when it should, or acts defectively, incurable civil disorders are seen to follow. Likewise, unscrupulous men of power—whose breed, alas, grows in every age and place like cockle among the wheat—take advantage of the weak for their own wicked gain. . . . .

66. As the interlocking organizations of modern society develop, right order will be realized more and more through a renewed balance between a demand for autonomous and active collaboration on the part of all—individuals and groups—and timely co-ordination and encouragement of private enterprise by government.

III

The appearance of the term *socialization* in the English translation of *Mater et Magistra* has caused great consternation in American Catholic and non-Catholic circles. The reason for this dismay, however, is merely a too hasty reading of the text and the apparent but false connotations of the term. As such, the term *socialization* does not appear in the Latin text, but it does appear in all modern language editions of the encyclical which were published on the same day as the Latin. Interestingly enough, the Italian text was undoubtedly the Pope's original, and the one which must be compared with the Latin for clarification. Like all other modern language texts, the Italian contained the word *socialization*. The problem that the word poses does not necessitate any detailed analysis of the question of translation: it should simply make clear at the outset that the term *socialization* does not mean *socialism,* and that the concept of *socialization* is an important key to understanding *Mater et Magistra.*

In presenting the reality of socialism, Pope John summarizes the position of his predecessor, Pius XI:

> 34. The Pope emphasizes, next, that the opposition between communism and Christianity is a fundamental one. He also makes it clear that Catholics can in no way give approval to the tenets of those who support a form of moderate socialism. The reason is that the Socialists look on the social order and human life as being bounded by time; this leads them to take as their exclusive objective man's welfare on earth. Moreover, because this theory views the social structure as being designed solely for production, it leads to an excessive restriction of human liberty and the abandonment of every sound principle of social authority.

Here it is important to note the three conditions of socialism mentioned by the Pope: the social order is exclusively temporal, its total object is nothing more than man's temporal good, and, finally, the abandonment of any sound notion of social authority. Obviously no Catholic, or no Christian for that matter, could consent to such a view of social order. It must be added, however, that any social order—capitalism included—which fulfills this definition would come under the ban of proscription no matter what its name. The important thing to remember is that realities be identified, and not simply names.[4]

Pope John, however, uses the term *socialization* in the sense that modern sociologists use it, namely, as a type of global and universal interaction of persons and of

---

[4] Cf. P. Riga, *Peace on Earth* (New York, 1964), pp. 178–182.

things. The concept involves a complicated intertwining of many and varied relationships in the economic, social and technological fields. Since these impersonal relationships affect all nations and peoples, men have become socially dependent on each other in a great number of institutions and associations. This dependency manifests itself in many ways in each of these fields, especially in the economic and industrial complex. These relationships are what might be called *elements of fact* which have united mankind in a unity never before thought possible.

The Pope puts it clearly when he specifies the three fields of politics, economy and culture. In connection with the process of socialization he states:

47. A glance at the fields of science, technology and economics reveals the following recent developments: the discovery of nuclear energy, its use in the first place for military purposes and now its increasing employment for peaceful ends; the unlimited possibilities opened up by chemistry in the production of synthetic goods; the wider use of machinery and automation in the areas of manufacturing and services; the modernization of agriculture; the virtual annihilation of the distances separating peoples by the new communications media, especially radio and television; the increased speed in all modes of transportation; and the initial conquests of interplanetary space.

48. If we turn our attention to the social field, we see the following developments: the formation of systems of social insurance and, in some more economically advanced states, the introduction of comprehensive social security systems; in labor unions the formation of, and increasing stress on,

an attitude of responsibility toward major socio-
economic problems; a progressive improvement of
basic education; an ever wider distribution of welfare benefits; increased social mobility with a con-
sequent lessening of class distinctions; a greater
interest in world events on the part of those with an
average education.

Furthermore, the increased efficiency of economic systems in a growing number of states
underscores the lack of socio-economic balance
between agriculture on the one hand and manufacturing and services on the other; between economically developed and less developed areas within
individual states; and, on a world-wide plane, the
even more pronounced socio-economic inequalities
among nations of different economic advantage.

49. Similarly, when one examines the political
field, a host of innovations come to light: in many
states, a participation in public life by an increasing
number of citizens from different social strata;
more frequent and extensive intervention by public
authorities in the economic and social fields. To
these developments must be added, on the international level, the passing of colonial regimes and the
attainment of political independence by the
peoples of Asia and Africa; the increase of close
relations between peoples and a deepening of their
interdependence; the emergence and development
of a supranational network of organizations having
a world-wide scope and pursuing economic, social,
cultural or common political ends.

Communication relays in space make possible an
almost instantaneous reporting of news in every part of
the globe. Because the world's economic life has be-

come interdependent through a more diversified demand for goods and raw materials, countries today must plan their economic life in relation to that of other countries. Science and technology have become international endeavors with no national boundaries. Culture itself is becoming worldwide. While each country retains and develops its proper genius, it is enriched by absorbing various elements from other cultures. All of these technological, economic, and cultural changes have been of great service in advancing civilization, that is, a greater sharing, on a global basis, of the common patrimony of all men by all men. History never before knew anything like this intensification which began with the Industrial Revolution and has been continuing at a breathtaking pace.

Yet, while these changes have had a profound influence on the social life of modern man, they can also have some stultifying effects on the free initiative and liberty of man. Pope John does not hesitate to give his recommendations to avoid the disadvantages of this modern phenomenon.

There are two ways in which the dangers of rapid change can be avoided. First, the Pope encourages the establishment and growth of intermediary groups and bodies which will assume the freedom of initiative, and which, as a result, will be conducive to the freedom of individuals. The value of these particular bodies (especially unions) and their importance have already been discussed under the principle of subsidiarity. The encouragement of intermediary groups is not sufficient. Because rapid technological developments have made the modern situation so complicated, these intermediary groups are limited in their power and capacity. The result is an impeding and progressive restriction of the initiative and freedom of individuals which comes in the wake of technological change. The wealth of power necessary to cope with this problem of regulation is ultimately lodged in the public authority, whose aim is the common good of all citizens. Of necessity, the powers of government must enlarge to meet the complicated problems of the intensified interaction of groups within society. The public authority, then, should regulate, control, and orientate this complicated process. Governmental regulation may even go as far as nationalization of vital industries if the common good truly demands it. Pius XII explicitly made this point in many of his allocutions and, thus, the added and more complicated role of public authority simply cannot be abandoned nor avoided in the industrialized society of the 1960's.

According to John XXIII, both intermediary groups and government must participate if society is to remain as free as possible for each of its citizens. If the state attempts to regulate everything and thereby destroy free, intermediary bodies, an immoral regime called totalitarianism arises; if the whole sphere of economic and social affairs is abandoned to private groups, the strong crush the weak and society returns to the chaos of a nineteenth-century economic liberalism with all of the attendant abuses of *laissez-faire*. In practice, a correct balance between the two is difficult to achieve and maintain. In underdeveloped countries, for example, the role of the state as economic and social co-ordinator will be greater because of a lack of formed and responsible intermediary business and union groups. On the other hand, these well-formed intermediary groups in economically advanced countries often pose the problem of monopoly which stifles the initiative and freedom of other citizens.

Thus, the Pope says, "socialization is one of the char-

acteristic features of our epoch" (par. 59). It has been
brought about by the application of advanced technology to modern society as well as other factors already
cited. Historically, the Industrial Revolution has resulted in the urbanization of the world's population. In
1966, for example, 80 per cent of the American population live in metropolitan areas; the tendency is also
growing rapidly in Asia and Latin America. This characteristic shift from the farm to the city arises from the
demands of an industrialized society, demands which
range from the concentration of a labor force to the easy
access to transportation for raw materials and finished
products. Since this complicated interdependency of
peoples affects man's powers to work out his own destiny, the natural right of association has become more
apparent and necessary. The growth of state power is
both an effect and a cause of this natural process, and, as
such, the Holy Father recognizes it as an immense
good.

> 60. Socialization is, at one and the same time, an
> effect and a cause of the growing intervention of
> the state in areas which, since they touch the
> deepest concerns of the human person, are not
> without considerable importance nor devoid of
> danger. Among these are care of health, instruction
> and education of the young, control of professional
> careers, methods of care and rehabilitation of those
> physically or mentally handicapped in any way.
> Socialization, however, is also the fruit and expres-
> sion of a natural tendency almost irrepressible in
> human beings—the tendency to unite for the pur-
> pose of obtaining objectives which each ambitions
> but which are beyond the capacity of individu-
> als.

This sort of tendency has given rise, especially in these latter decades, to a wide range of groups, associations and institutions having economic, cultural, social, athletic, recreational, professional and political ends. They operate within a single nation and on a world-wide basis.

The good which comes from socialization is manifested concretely in the extension and development of man's natural rights in health, education and welfare (see *Pacem in terris,* par. 11–13, 18–22). Grants by the state, scholarships of all kinds, public education, and other educational endeavors help promote the natural right of man to develop his talents. Group insurance, social security, compensation, health insurance, and minimal professional competency have given modern man a sense of security never before enjoyed on the earth. These benefits and others are the result of socialization, which is occurring nationally and internationally.

61. [Socialization] makes possible, in fact, the satisfaction of many personal rights, especially those of a socio-economic nature. The right to the indispensable means of human subsistence, to health services, to instruction at a higher level, to more thorough professional formation, to housing, to employment, to suitable leisure and to decent recreation are typical examples. In addition, through increasing systematization of modern media of mass communications—press, motion pictures, radio, television—it becomes possible for individuals to participate, as it were, in human events even on a world-wide scale.

It is now a commonplace to say that the world has

become smaller in size, in communication, in trade, and thus it has become interdependent; this growing socialization of society must now indeed be termed international.

Pope John does not deny that there are distinct disadvantages to the process of socialization. The individual's freedom of initiative is restricted, and government interferes in many intimate aspects of a man's life.

> 62. At the same time, however, socialization multiplies institutional structures and extends more and more to minute details and juridical control of human relations in every walk of life. As a consequence, it restricts the range of an individual's freedom of action. It uses means, follows methods and creates an atmosphere which make it difficult for one to reach judgments free from external pressures, to work on his own initiative, to exercise responsibility and to assert his personality.

The great danger here is depersonalization, the supreme bane of human society. Workers in industry become cogs, welfare recipients become cases, neighbors in housing projects become absolute strangers, Social Security becomes a number, the government becomes a great bureaucracy which controls and regulates by unfeeling laws. Liberty of initiative and independence of action become stifled and each person's responsibility becomes limited. In the United States, certain elements in the population, calling themselves conservative, have sensed these disadvantages and, in reaction to them, have branded any governmental interference a reduction of freedom. Undoubtedly, the above disadvantages are real and must be carefully considered in building and planning the social order. Unlike the so-called conservatives, the Holy Father is fundamentally optimistic about the modern world. He knows that socialization and stronger governmental powers do not necessarily mean a diminution of freedom and responsibility, because the advantages of socialization can offset its disadvantages.

> 64. Accordingly, advances in social organization can and should be so brought about that the maximum advantages accrue to citizens while at the same time disadvantages are averted or at least minimized.

Since man is a free being, that which he has brought about in freedom can be controlled, and so any disadvantage which arises in the social system can be held to a minimum. In a very real sense, man has in fact been freed from the slavery of fate by socialization. Health insurances and such programs as Medicare have freed men from the instabilities of health; Social Security, from the economic infirmities of old age; automation, from the slavery of back-breaking toil; communications, from the restrictions of time and space. In short, man is "not forced to become an automaton": just as socialization was and is the product of man's free will and initiative, by that same free will he can control and humanize the disadvantages of socialization.

Since these disadvantages affect the individual, they are best offset by the efforts of both the public authority and of private groups and intermediate bodies. Private charity organizations such as the Catholic Charities, the Jewish Relief Fund, and the World Council of Churches do solid work in conjunction with public welfare agencies. The efforts of such private agencies keep welfare, assistance, and retraining on a more personal and, therefore, more human level. To issue checks to welfare recipients is not enough, because it merely perpetuates and hardens poverty. The great need is for the personal concern of social case workers, psychologists, forward-looking architects and planners for humanized urban renewal, and men who know that the reintegration of the poor and disadvantaged into the viable society must also restore their sense of hope and dignity. Too often welfare programs are looked upon as public doles, but such a view perpetuates an inhuman concept of this work among the poor, the racial groups, the aged, and the culturally deprived.[5] To remain human, according to Pope John, the object of welfare must be to remove people from the relief rolls and restore them back to productivity, where they will once again regain the responsibility for their own fate and destiny.

Contrary to many social scientists and self-appointed "prophets of doom," the Pope does not see increased organization and government regulation as opposed to individual freedom; on the contrary, socialization is in itself a great blessing since it brings in its wake the fulfillment of many human rights which formerly went unfulfilled because of the primitive conditions of society.

> 67. So long as socialization is kept within these limits of the moral order, it will not of its nature seriously restrict individuals or overburden them. Instead, it offers hope of promoting in them the expression and development or their personal characteristics. It results, too, in an organic reconstruction of society, which Our predecessor Pius XI in *Quadragesimo Anno,* put forward and defended as the indispensable prerequisite for satisfying abundantly the demands of social justice.

[5] E. May, *The Wasted Americans* (New York, 1963), p. 37.

The Holy Father envisions this happy result on condition that public officials view the common good as that which is most favorable to the development of the human personality. Society is a community of persons, not of automatons or individuals brain-washed by propaganda or by an exorbitant desire for material things. The Pope summed this up concisely and pointedly in *Pacem in terris,* where he said:

> 36. Human society, Venerable Brothers and beloved children, ought to be regarded above all as a spiritual reality in which men communicate knowledge to each other in the light of truth, in which they can enjoy their rights and fulfill their duties, and are inspired to strive for moral good. Society should enable men to share in and enjoy every legitimate expression of beauty, and encourage them constantly to pass on to others all that is best in themselves, while they strive to make their own the spiritual achievements of others. These are the spiritual values which continually give life and basic orientation to cultural expressions, economic and social institutions, political movements and forms, laws, and all other structures by which society is outwardly established and constantly developed.

Intermediate Groups
and Unions

I

POPE JOHN'S PERSONALISTIC VIEW of a balanced and just
society is one in which the citizens themselves participate as fully as possible in social and economic functions. Such participation gives each citizen a feeling of
importance and responsibility *vis-à-vis* society itself,
and it makes society more humane and more in conformity with the innate dignity of the human person.[1]
Since the natural right of such an organization has been
part and parcel of Catholic social thought from the time
of *Rerum Novarum,* the principal way to achieve the
humanized society is for citizens to organize into small,
personal groups for economic and social activity. The
Pope applies the right to organize more extensively.
Unions, mutuals, various types of cooperatives in the
economy such as agricultural and professional organizations, are singled out for special consideration. Because
these groups permit citizens to have an organized
influence on the economic life of society, their participation in it has a more humane influence on its organization. They are ruled by their own laws, and, often, their

[1] See par. 55, 61–62, 83–84, 91, 94, 96, 99, 112, 118, 154, 161,
182, 197, 205, 244, 256, 259.

problems become national problems. Labor unions, for example, have posed many problems for the consideration of the public authority, and the result has been a special branch of jurisprudence called labor law. Thus the Holy Father says with regard to these groups:

> 65. That these desired objectives may be more readily obtained, it is necessary that public authorities have a correct understanding of the common good. This embraces the sum total of those conditions of social living, whereby men are enabled more fully and more readily to achieve their own perfection. Hence, we regard it as necessary that the various intermediary bodies and the numerous social undertakings wherein an expanded social structure primarily finds expression, be ruled by their own laws, and as the common good itself progresses, pursue this objective in a spirit of sincere concord among themselves. Nor is it less necessary that the above-mentioned groups present the form and substance of a true community. This they will do only if individual members are considered and treated as persons, and are encouraged to participate in the affairs of the group.

Since the individual's effect on modern society has become almost negligible, and since modern society has become infinitely complicated in its socialized structures, only through organization can the individual effectively influence it, thus acting responsibly toward it. Obviously, the Pope sees society as a corporate unity where each sector depends upon and, in turn, influences other sectors.

One of the clearest examples of individuals organizing for effective responsible action is the labor union. Leo XIII gave the workingman a special mandate by

teaching him that labor unions were a natural right;
Pope John XXIII gives this economic and social activity
an even more forceful inculcation and justification. The
Popes' encouragement of labor is in clear contrast to the
"anti-union" sentiment which is again in vogue in many
Western countries, especially in the United States.
While there is no need here to give a detailed history of
the labor movement's struggle for survival and recognition, it should be remembered that certain economic
conservatives of the nineteenth and twentieth century
have never forgiven labor for its successful rise. Not so
the Pope. He not only justifies unions but wants them to
take a more active part in the management of industry
itself. He argues that industry is the product of the work
of both labor and management, and so its profits ought
to be shared by both in a type of effective co-partnership. Beyond this, he encourages labor unions to make
their voices and forces felt not only in the economy but
also in civic community. With the benefits of modern
technology and socialization, the worker has become
more cognizant of his rights as a citizen and, therefore,
of his responsibilities to the total society in which he
lives. Because society has so large an influence on the
worker, he must have the power as well as the right to
make his voice felt in its formation. The Pope makes this
need very clear:

> 99. But it is not the decisions made within each
> individual productive unit which have the greatest
> bearing on this complex. Instead, it is those made
> by public authorities, or by institutions that func-
> tion on a world-wide or national scale in regard to
> some economic sector or category of production.
> Hence it is appropriate and necessary that, besides

the holders of capital or their representatives, the workers also, or those who represent their rights, demands and aspirations, should have some place in such authorities or institutions.

By recommending such participation in the highest decision-making areas of society, the Pope thereby expands both the vision as well as the influence of the worker. This right of the working man to participate in society was more clearly stated in *Pacem in terris* (especially par. 26); there, Pope John reminds workers that through their natural right to take part in government they can influence their society. Though worker participation in both political and economic democracy was clearly elaborated in Pius XII's Christmas Message of 1941, the two social encyclicals of John XXIII emphasize this aspect of participation more forcibly. Later in *Mater et Magistra,* the Pope extends this right and obligation to the rural areas of the world, for in his total view of society, the Pope realizes that every worker, rural and urban, must share the benefits and the responsibilites in order to achieve his complete fulfillment.

The basis for worker participation in society is given in capsule form in three paragraphs of *Pacem in terris:*

> 11. Beginning our discussion of the rights of man, we see that every man has the right to life, to bodily integrity, and to the means which are necessary and suitable for the proper development of life; these are primarily food, clothing, shelter, rest, medical care, and finally the necessary social services. Therefore a human being also has the right to security in case of sickness, inability to work, widowhood, old age, unemployment, or in any

other case in which he is deprived of the means of subsistence through no fault of his own.

12. By the natural law every human being has the right to respect for his person, to his good reputation; the right to freedom in searching for truth and in expressing and communicating his opinions, and in pursuit of art, within the limits laid down by the moral order and the common good; and he has the right to be informed truthfully about public events.

13. The natural law also gives man the right to share in the benefits of culture, and therefore the right to a basic education and to technical and professional training in keeping with the stage of educational development in the country to which he belongs. Every effort should be made to ensure that persons be enabled, on the basis of merit, to go on to higher studies, so that, as far as possible, they may occupy posts and take on responsibilities in human society in accordance with their natural gifts and the skills they have acquired.

Such worker participation presupposes a complete program of social reform in any particular country. In some, the levels of production and the degree of participation in the culture are more advanced than in others; yet, here, as in *Pacem in terris,* the Pope has presented a social ideal. In some economically underdeveloped countries, the level of participation possible for each individual in the culture will necessarily be less. The Pope will note this when he discusses the underdeveloped countries in Part Three of *Mater et Magistra.*[2]

According to John XXIII, one of the best ways of implementing this program of total participation—

[2] See above, pp. 142–191.

especially in industrial societies—is by the intermediary bodies of working men called unions. Because they are sources of freedom in truly free society, dictatorships of any kind—whether of the right or of the left—crush the trade union movement in the country. As recent history under Hitler, Mussolini, Lenin, and Franco has proved, free trade unions can exist only in an environment where democratic processes allow a free government to prevail under the direction of a free people. The surest indications and guarantees of a free society are free intermediate groups, paramount of which are free and protected trade unions. The mind of the Pope in this matter is clear. In making this point, Pope John repeats the teaching of Leo XIII:

> 22. The encyclical declares that the right of workers alone, or of groups of both workers and owners, to organize is a natural one. The same is said about the right to adopt that organizational structure which the workers consider most suitable to promote their legitimate occupational interests, and the right to act freely, without hindrance from anyone, and on their own initiative—within the associations—to achieve these ends.

Unions are not only morally just, but they are a necessity for the working and professional classes.[3] In our highly socialized technological society, such organization is a moral imperative both in the economically developed and underdeveloped countries.

There is one striking factor in the Pope's discussion of labor unions which ought not go unnoticed. In paragraphs 100–103, the discussion progresses from Christian labor unions to neutral ones, and finally to those

[3] G. C. Higgins, "The Meaning of 'Mater et Magistra,'" *Ave Maria*, 94 (August, 1961), p. 8.

which attempt to internationalize workers' rights
(ILO):

100. Our affectionate thought, therefore, and
our paternal encouragement go out with all pro-
priety to professional groups and workers' associations founded on Christian principles and existing
and functioning on more than one continent. In the
midst of many and frequently grave difficulties,
these, Our sons, have been striving and continue to
strive for the effective promotion of the interests of
the working classes and for their material and
moral improvement. This they do within the area of
a single political unity as well as on an international
scale.

101. Moreover, we wish to single out for praise
the fact that their work is not directed exclusively
to immediate and visible results, but to the world
wide field of human toil, where it spreads correctly
orientated principles and furnishes a stimulus to
Christian reform.

102. We believe further that one must praise in
the same way the outstanding endeavors performed in a true Christian spirit by our beloved
sons in other professional groups and workers' associations which take their inspiration from natural
law principles and show respect for freedom of
conscience.

103. We are also happy to express our heartfelt
appreciation to the International Labor Organization (ILO), which for decades has been making its
effective and precious contribution to the establishment in the world of a socio-economic order
marked by justice and humanity and one in which
the lawful demands of the workers are recognized
and defended.

These paragraphs indicate a sort of evolution in Catholic thought.[4] For the first time in a pontifical document, praise is given to the so-called "neutral" labor unions, that is, unions whose direct inspiration is not Christian principles, but rather the demands of natural law for social and international justice. These demands of natural law are particularly obvious in the general spirit of the International Labor Organization of the United Nations. The Pope's positive encouragement of such unions and labor organizations make them acceptable areas in which the Catholic can work.

Because Leo XIII had proposed "moral and religious perfection" as the principal object of labor union membership, its achievement was possible only in Christian labor unions, thus limiting the value of other types of unions for Catholics. Leo XIII's insistence on this object caused the Vatican to suspect the Knights of Labor, which flourished in the United States at the turn of the century. Like all major unions which have developed in the United States, the Knights was a "neutral" union. It should be remembered, however, that Cardinal Gibbons was able to convince Leo XIII that the Knights of Labor was pursuing good ends and the result was that Catholics were allowed to participate. Pius XI also believed that Catholics ought to band together in Catholic labor unions for the principal purpose of religious and moral betterment. However, the progressive realization that many labor unions are founded on the desire for social justice has led to an expansion of this view in pontifical documents from 1891 to 1961. Paralleling this evolution, the American bishops in their annual statements have also indicated an enlarging view of labor unions. Thus in *Mater et Magistra,* neutral unions are not only recognized as possible outlets for good, but

[4] O. Nell-B-R-euning, "Mater et Magistra," *Stimmen der Zeit,* 87 (Nov., 1961), pp. 116–128.

they are actually praised and encouraged. All three types of unions—Catholic, neutral, and international—are given equal praise in their aims for social justice and freedom of conscience.

Though it may seem—at least in appearance—that the union sentiments of *Mater et Magistra* are different from those expressed by Leo XIII and Pius XI, the reality has not changed in the least. After all, the desire of the Church is for her children to achieve social justice, and also to protect them from alien philosophies which have often infected labor movements. The European labor movement has been more susceptible to these alien philosophies, but even the United States has had these problems. Until the early thirties, for example, the Communists attempted to gain control of the United States labor movement. But, happily, the United States has not fallen into the ideological struggles which have plagued and continue to plague the European labor movement, and American Catholics have not been forced to form their own unions to avoid infection. From the time of Samuel Gompers and the founding of the A.F. of L., American labor unions have been "bread and butter" unions, fighting for just wages and better working conditions, and they have steered clear of such notions as deterministic materialism, the denial of private property, or class hatred. There have been conflicts in American unionism, but they have never turned on ideology. Even when John L. Lewis broke with the A.F. of L. in the 30's and founded the C.I.O., the ideological struggle, if it can be called that, was a matter of extending Gomper's "bread and butter" concept to the millions of workers who, properly speaking, had no trade—that is, to the industrial workers who were semi-skilled or unskilled. Since the end of World War II the ideological problems which have beset the European labor movement have been resolved to such a degree that the Pope can include it in his praise.

The values represented by the world labor movement are, by and large, dictated by the principles of natural law and social justice which Catholics hold in common with non-Catholic Christians and non-Christians. As part and parcel of the *magisterium* which alone is able to discern philosophical and moral error in the social order, the Holy See determines when an evolution of thought, such as that toward the labor movement, has come about. The Church cannot remain indifferent to any and every objective of labor unions, so she must judge these objectives in the light of the moral and natural law, and the authority to form this judgment is lodged in both the Holy See and local episcopal assemblies. Because the conditions of labor in each particular country will vary, the judgment of local episcopacies is very important. In the final analysis, however, it is the laymen in the Church who, enlightened by the proper authority, are responsible for implementing this social doctrine within the contingencies of time and place. Thus, the continuous dialogue between laymen and bishops takes on greater immediacy. The bishops must be fully informed about practical situations, and this can only be done by laymen. In this sense, laymen, with the bishops and the Pope, share in the pastoral office of the Church. As the Pope clearly points out in the last section of *Mater et Magistra,* laymen are directly responsible for the social mission of the Church in the world.

II

The early struggle of the American labor union movement was centered in what has been called the "bread and butter" needs of workers. This pragmatic program of labor was achieved through two basic instruments: organization and the "strike." In the past and in the present, a just wage and safe working conditions are absolutely essential for the well-being of the working and professional classes, and then as now, the chief safeguard for these basic needs has been the labor union. Yet the effort by certain employers, state legislatures, and national political figures to pass and enforce right-to-work laws is indirectly calculated to destroy, or at least to diminish, the bargaining power of labor unions by outlawing the union shop. In effect, such laws override the principle of majority rule because the workers are forbidden to elect whether they want their "shop" organized. This agitation for right-to-work laws is alarming, for, in modern society, labor is powerless without organization. More specifically, these laws are fundamentally immoral because the interest groups that promote them intend to hinder the only reasonable process by which the worker can achieve his just reward.

One of the prominent political figures in this country, Barry M. Goldwater, wishes to see the prompt enactment of right-to-work laws. "These laws," he says, "are aimed at removing a great blight on the contemporary American scene, and I am at a loss to understand why so many people who so often profess concern for 'civil rights' and 'civil liberties' are vehemently opposed to them. Freedom of association is one of the natural rights of man. Clearly, therefore, it should also be a 'civil' right. Right-to-work laws derive from the natural law: they are simply an attempt to give freedom of association the added protection of civil law."[5] The case is stated clearly enough and the matter is quite serious for two reasons: first, Goldwater claims that such laws are

[5] *The Conscience of a Conservative* (New York, 1963), p. 50.

derived from the natural law and therefore are basically moral in content (right of association);[6] and second, every eminent Catholic social thinker in this country believes the opposite, that is, that the so-called right-to-work laws, in the overall view, are basically incompatible with the moral law and therefore immoral.

The term "right to work" is, in reality, a misnomer. In all cases the basic intent of such laws is to resist union organization. In 1954, the Idaho Supreme Court took note of this intention and refused to permit so deceptive a name for an initiative measure to be proposed to the voters. The phrase certainly ought not to be confused with what the Church and, in particular, Pope John calls "the right to work." "Human beings," the Pope says, "have the natural right to free initiative in the economic field, and the right to work" (*Pacem in terris,* par. 18). A man has the right of free initiative because of his originality and irreplaceability. From this follows man's right and obligation to work so that he can make his contribution to society. In this discussion, *work* is to be understood in its broadest sense: it is not just financially productive activities, but every activity which promotes all aspects of a culture. It is a noble thing; and, as modern theologians have put it, work is a furthering of God's creating act. The fruition of culture through work is therefore a social task in which everyone must make his contribution according to his capacities. Since all men have the duty to promote culture through work, this same duty is therefore the basis of man's right to work. Man's work is his contribution, and by it he should be able to earn what is necessary for him to maintain his dignity and that of his family. According to papal teaching, the right to work is a personal right, but the state also has a definite role to play in promoting it.

[6] See *Pacem in terris,* par. 23.

The state must help create the conditions and milieu favorable to work and productivity so that "full employment" will be as much a reality as possible in any particular society. One of the essential functions of the state must be to promote the economic life of its citizens: "It is therefore necessary that the administration give whole-hearted and careful attention to the social as well as the economic progress of its citizens, and to the development in keeping with the development of the productive system, of such essential services as the building of roads, transportation, communication, water supply, housing, public health. . . . It is necessary also that governments make efforts to see that insurance systems are made available to the citizens so that in case of misfortune or increased family responsibilities, no person will be without the necessary means to maintain a decent way of living. The government should make similarly effective efforts to see that those who are able to work can find employment in keeping with their aptitudes, and that each worker receives a wage in keeping with the laws of justice and equity" (*Pacem in terris,* par. 64). Thus, the meaning of "the right to work" in papal literature is not in any way the same as that of American right-to-work laws. The latter is a particular American phenomenon, reference to which is made neither in the social encyclicals nor in any of the statements of the American hierarchy.

The right of labor unions to organize is basic to the thought of *Mater et Magistra.* As the Pope observes, "Today almost nobody hears, much less pays attention to isolated voices" (par. 146). The Pope is very clear on this point:

> The encyclical declares that the right of workers alone, or of groups of both workers and owners, to

organize is a natural one. The same is said about the right to adopt that organizational structure which the workers consider most suitable to promote their legitimate occupational interests, and the right to act freely, without hindrance from anyone, and on their own initiative—within the associations—to achieve these ends. (Par. 22.)

The purpose of unions is to promote the rights of workers both on a national and international plane (par. 101–103). To accomplish this end, collective bargaining is labor's supreme instrument:

Now it is evident to all that in our day associations of workers have become widespread, and for the most part have been given legal status within individual countries and even across natural boundaries. These bodies no longer recruit workers for the purposes of strife, but rather for pursuing a common aim. And this is achieved especially by collective bargaining between associations of workers and those of management. (Par. 97.)

The Pope approves unions because they are a necessary means which proceeds from the natural law ("a natural right") and, as such, their formation and function comes under the moral and binding teaching of the Holy Father. This can be disputed by no Catholic nor by anyone who holds to the tradition of the natural law. The Pope's attitude is a far cry from that of many Americans who protest that unions have become too powerful, too corrupt, and who propose their restraint and, by right-to-work laws, their gradual elimination as a strong power at the bargaining table. The Pope does not mention right-to-work laws, but it is hard to see how these laws can be reconciled with the spirit of the Pope's teaching on labor unions.

A right-to-work law is defined as legislation which forbids an employer to force an employee to be or to become a member in a union. In short, such laws forbid both closed and union shops. A closed shop is a situation in which the employer may hire only union members; a union shop allows the employer to hire non-union members, but they must become union members after a specified period of time. The Taft-Hartley Act of 1947 legally banned the closed shop, while the union shop is permitted only if the majority of the members of an enterprise wish it. If 30 percent of the workers so stipulate, the National Labor Relations Board must hold a secret ballot to determine if the majority wants to end the union shop. This stipulation has back-fired. In 1951, Congress repealed this clause of the law for the obvious reason that the employees had amply shown their satisfaction and approval of the union shop to represent them in collective bargaining. "In 46,119 elections conducted by the NLRB between August, 1947, and October, 1951, more than 5 million votes were cast for the union shop. That was 91 percent of all the votes cast. In 97.1 percent of the elections the workers authorized the Union shops."[7] The law, however, by repealing this clause, permitted the states to go beyond the Taft-Hartley Act and forbid the union shop. There can be little doubt that the intent and the practical consequences of these laws have been to weaken unions and their functions in society.

Obviously, then, the right-to-work laws dangerously weaken the essential bargaining power of labor unions. Yet, the argument remains to be answered. Mr. Goldwater argues that such laws proceed from the natural law of the right of association. This right is indeed a natural one and if this were the only consideration

[7] B. Masse, *Justice For All* (Milwaukee, 1964), p. 113.

involved here, the case for the right-to-work laws would be settled in their favor. Yet, there is also the natural right to organize in order to obtain economic justice through collective bargaining. These two natural laws appear to be in conflict but, in fact, they come in conflict only when stated as mutually exclusive. But they are not that, and Mr. Goldwater does the nation a disservice when he states them as such.

As all Catholic social thinkers have emphasized, man is a social being. He develops himself as an individual only to the degree that he works and cooperates with others in a common task. Always condemning the two extremes of individualism and collectivism, Christian truth stands between the two. Yet herein lies the paradox. Freedom in human relations is never complete and absolute. When a man enters into communion with other men, he is bound to respect their rights (freedom to organize), but they are also bound to respect his right to choose (freedom of association). It becomes immediately evident that neither of these two rights can be an absolute, because one is bound by the other. The solution lies in recognizing that human nature and rights are inherently limited by the human condition and that each situation must be examined to determine how human freedom can be maximized and how limitations to human freedom can be minimized. The Holy Father states this clearly in *Mater et Magistra:*

> But as these various forms of association are multiplied and daily extended, it also happens that in many areas of activity, rules and laws controlling and determining relationships of citizens are multiplied. As a consequence, opportunity for free action by individuals is restricted within narrower limits. Methods are often used, procedures are

adopted, and such an atmosphere develops wherein it becomes difficult for one to make decisions independently of outside influences, to do anything on his own initiative, to carry out in a fitting way his rights and duties, and to fully develop and perfect his personality. Will men perhaps, then, become automatons, and cease to be personally responsible, as these social relationships multiply more and more? It is a question which must be answered negatively.

Actually, increased complexity of social life by no means results from a blind drive of natural forces. Indeed, as stated above, it is the creation of free men who are so disposed to act by nature as to be responsible for what they do. They must, of course, recognize the laws of human progress and the development of economic life and take these into account. Furthermore, men are not altogether free of their milieu.

Accordingly, advances in social organization can and should be so brought about that maximum advantages accrue to citizens while at the same time disadvantages are averted or at least minimized. (Par. 62–64.)

A close examination of the right-to-work laws reveals that the delicate balance between these two natural rights is not kept. The right of association is so stressed that the right of organization for bargaining is destroyed. Forbidding the union shop when the workers themselves will it is a flagrant violation of the natural right of association. Such laws deprive the workers in any particular industry of collective bargaining strength; without this strength, which comes from a voluntary association in labor unions, workers are left to

the mercy of powerful economic forces which any industry or group of industries can employ. As the Pope
has already indicated (par. 146), individual voices in
modern organized societies do not have much power
against the gigantic force of industrial and economic
interests. Any law which would weaken the bargaining
power of labor organizations can only be branded as
immoral. Such are the right-to-work laws.

The argument against right-to-work laws is clear, but
many Catholic thinkers go much further. In the above
argument, the demand for "voluntary" associations of
workers was purposely mentioned, and the fact that
American unions are voluntary is eminently proved by
the results of the NLRB's secret union elections between
1947 and 1951. Many Catholic social thinkers go further. Given the complexity of modern society, workers
have a moral obligation to join a union in order to attain
economic justice, because organizational power is necessary for effective collective bargaining. The argument
is sound enough, but it ought not be made so absolute as
to exclude such measures as the "agency shop," where
workers in a particular industry pay regular dues and
entrust the local union to bargain for them, but for one
reason or another, do not wish to join a labor union.
Sometimes this reluctance to join a union is caused by
religious scruples, and this freedom ought to be given to
local workers as long as the essential bargaining power
of the union is not threatened. In the words of the
bishops of Quebec Province (February, 1950):

> Every man has an obligation to seek to protect the
> security of his professional interests. He has the
> duty to seek to obtain for himself and his family all
> that is necessary in order to live a truly human life
> and to safeguard them against human hazards. He

has the duty to contribute to the welfare of his fellows, especially those united to him in common interests. He has the duty to collaborate in restoring a social order which would be more balanced in favoring respect for justice in all the activities of labor, industry and commerce. The isolated worker cannot do this. But union with his fellow workers will permit him to fulfill this imperious social duty. In the present state of things, accordingly, there exists a moral obligation to participate actively in one's economic organization.

Curiously, it is not the worker who decries his lack of "freedom" in union membership. On the national level, the principal sponsors of such laws are the National Association of Manufacturers, the United States Chamber of Commerce, and the National Right to Work Committee. This is not surprising. The NAM's history of opposition to the union shop dates back to 1908. The terms have changed, not the reality. In 1908, the closed shop was known as the "open shop," but its purpose was the same. To this group must be added many of the organizations of the right wing, whose opposition to labor unions verges on fanaticism. This is indeed a strange group of bedfellows who are very "worried" about the freedom of unions.

The states where such laws exist also arouse a suspicion as to the real motives of their enactment: anti-union warfare. Nineteen states have such laws on their books: Alabama, Arizona, Arkansas, Florida, Georgia, Indiana, Iowa, Kansas, Mississippi, Nebraska, Nevada, North Carolina, North Dakota, South Carolina, South Dakota, Tennessee, Texas, Utah, and Virginia. Louisiana has open shops applying to workers in agriculture and sugar processing. In these states, for the most part, the labor movement is weak, and it is here that organization is needed the most. Only one state, Indiana, can qualify as an industrial state. The reason for right-to-work laws in these states is obvious: cheap labor attracts business from the North, and these states, mostly in the South, want to prosper by industrialization. By such immoral laws, the cost production can be substantially cut, thus attracting business. Ironically enough, twelve of the above states have statutes establishing an "integrated bar," by which all lawyers are compelled by law to belong to their bar association. The same is true in many states with regard to the medical profession. It is only the labor union which is made the object of "freedom for its members." Turpitude of intent is obvious.

The main argument given by the proposers of such legislation is that it allows the individual the "freedom" to join or not to join a union. In reality, the idea of freedom forwarded in this argument is an exaggerated individualism which is applied, obviously, to trade unions, but not to the legal and the medical professions. But since a man is both individual and social, he has obligations to others which limit his individualism. Every individual right, in fact, is limited by a corresponding social responsibility, and this is clearly evident in Catholic social teaching. In a highly complex and industrialized society the voice of one man, as Pope John points out, is of little avail in correcting abuses and demanding just wages. He must of necessity organize into voluntary groups to exercise the power to make his demands known. Further, economic freedom for the worker lies in his ability to organize and in no other way. If the worker has the obligation to organize, he has the right to do so, and right-to-work laws which impede this right are immoral.

To reinstate a vanished nineteenth-century individualism for the worker is to leave him helpless and naked before the crushing demands of a superior economic force. The right of labor to organize has been accepted in all Catholic social circles from the days of the guilds, and it is indeed surprising that Catholic voices are heard in defense of right-to-work laws. The Archbishop of Hartford has declared:

> The sponsors of the proposed legislation claim that the fundamental right of the individual is invaded if he must join a union. I do not agree with this viewpoint. It is neither immoral nor unethical to require union membership for the greater common good of the group. In our modern and complex society, everyone is subject to prohibitions and restraints, as well as to mandatory rules of conduct based on the common good of the group.[8]

The very idea of collective bargaining is destroyed, in effect, by such legislation. If there is no union to represent the collective voices of the members of an enterprise, the "freedom" gained is the law of the economic jungle, ruled by the whim of superior economic force. Such a situation can only have disastrous consequences and cause the rebirth of the hateful class warfare prevalent in the nineteenth century, which, as Marx understood, prepares the way for communism. It is ironic that the right wing, so intent on anti-communism, would wish to bring about the conditions in our society which were principally responsible for the birth of communistic dynamism: class struggle. The bishops of Ohio put it this way:

> Man has a right and duty to work for his livelihood. This right cannot be circumscribed to the

[8] Reprint of NCWC News Service (Washington, D. C., March 20, 1958).

44

extent that a man loses his liberty of choice or a vocation; nor to the extent that he is deprived of an opportunity to support himself and his family. It does not follow that a man has the unconditional right to work in any and every industry or business at will.

For reasons of social justice it may be desirable and often advantageous to the common good that man's right be restricted by certain specified conditions. One of these imposed conditions may require that he belong to a labor union or at least be obliged to join the union subsequently, so as to share responsibility with his fellow workmen in support of the union. . . .

If state statutes were to make such a condition of union maintenance mandatory, we would oppose them as unwise, if not unjust. If state statutes however were to forbid the enforcement of such a condition, when mutually accepted by management and labor through collective bargaining, then we would be equally opposed.[9]

Archbishop Joseph F. Rummel of New Orleans put it this way:

It is a misnomer because it actually denies what it pretends to give, namely, the right to work.

It is reactionary because it nullifies all that has been accomplished in our State through the organized labor movement for the mutual benefit of working classes and the stability of industry.

It is insincere because, while it pretends to guarantee the right to work, it actually frustrates that right, in effect exposing labor to lose security, a decent standard of living, and humane working

[9] *Ibid.*

45

conditions. It makes a mockery of the constitutional right to organize for the common good and welfare. It invites continuing and recurring social strife and discontent. In a word, it is unfair and unsocial class legislation contrary to the common good.[10]

And finally, in a letter to the New York *Labor Leader* (April, 1955), Archbishop Robert E. Lucey of San Antonio stated it bluntly but accurately: "The efforts of certain evil interests to foist the fraudulent 'right-to-work' laws on the people of the several states is a sad commentary on their greed, selfishness and stupidity."

The right-to-work laws in the United States are therefore immoral in the intent, for the most part, of those seeking their enactment, and in their result, which is to destroy the delicate balance between the two equally basic rights of association and organization. This condemnation of right-to-work laws does not mean, however, that unions are everywhere and under all circumstances to be defended. From many points of view they have been and continue to be deficient. Labor corruption is a blight which must be eliminated by a more active participation of union members in the affairs of their locals. More Jimmy Hoffas can only bring disgrace on the labor movement as a whole. Yet abuses do not negate the essential and proper functions of unionization, and corruption in unions is not ended by weakening unions at their essential core: the strength of their bargaining power. Unions have other blights as well which need correction. Discrimination against minority groups particularly in the craft unions, for example, should be ended. In this respect, legislation such as Title II of the Civil Rights Act of 1964 is good, and

---

[10] B. Masse, *op. cit.*, pp. 119–120.

impartial enforcement of this clause will eliminate a real union abuse. To give another example, unions have failed to make a sustained effort in organizing people in those parts of the economy which most need it, such as hospital and migrant workers (one thinks here of the flagrant injustice done by the vegetable growers of California). The attitude of some union leaders toward these unfortunates is that of apathy and neglect. Yet, when all is said and done, the social philosophy and objectives of unions are still basically sound and in agreement with the social teachings of the Church. The same, however, cannot be said for the proponents of right-to-work laws.

III

Continuing his discussion of unions, the Pope proceeds to expand the role of workers. Labor, he insists, must concern itself not only with its private interests, but also with interests which affect the whole social body:

> 48. If we turn our attention to the social field, we see the following developments: the formation of systems of social insurance and, in some more economically advanced states, the introduction of comprehensive social security systems; in labor unions the formation of, and increasing stress on, an attitude of responsibility toward major socio-economic problems; progressive improvement of basic education; an even wider distribution of welfare benefits; increased social mobility with a consequent lessening of class distinctions; a greater interest in world events on the part of those with an average education. . . .
>
> 97. Modern times have seen a widespread in-

crease in worker associations organized with juridical status in many countries and across national lines. They no longer unite workers for the sake of conflict, but rather for joint effort—principally in the field of collective bargaining. But we cannot fail to emphasize how imperative or at least highly opportune it is that the workers should be able freely to make their voices heard, and listened to, beyond the confines of their individual productive units and at every level of society.

The Pope approves such participation, and in expanding his suggestions in paragraphs 97–103, he presents the most dynamic as well as the most daring part of the encyclical. His suggestions pass beyond "bread and butter" issues, and strike at the very heart of industrial organization. In the words of Pope John, the workers must proceed from a *work contract* ("bread and butter" issues such as just wages, vacations, health conditions, insurances, and so on) to a contract of open participation. In paragraph 32, he explains that Leo XIII believed in such power for the worker, and he assumes this power in the present encyclical. For Pope John, worker participation should ultimately end in a *contract of partnership* through such instruments as cooperatives, profit-sharing, shares and stocks in the company. In *Quadragesimo Anno,* Pope Pius XI had previously mentioned similar co-operation in industrial organization, and here Pope John gives the concept added emphasis. Following the established principle of Pius XI, Pope John does not claim that this kind of participation is a natural right. But he observes that Pius XI had strongly urged such worker participation, and, in paragraph 75 of *Mater et Magistra,* he suggests ways to implement this principle through self-financing by industry and workers, participation by shares, credits, and various other means of active direction and co-operation in the industry itself. Making the thought of Pius XI his own, Pope John insists that the product of any industry is never the result of one or the other party alone: it is the fruit of both the employer's and the employee's labor. When these aspects of the Pope's theology of work are considered the concept of *laissez-faire* capitalism is indirectly condemned, as is the theory that only the profit motive regulates industry. Because the workers are co-producers of the product, they are entitled to a greater profit for their labor; it must not all accrue to the owners of industry:

> 76. In this connection, We must recall the principle proposed by Our predecessor Pius XI in *Quadragesimo Anno*. *It is totally false to ascribe to capital alone or to labor alone that which is obtained by the joint effort of the one and the other. And it is flagrantly unjust that either should deny the efficacy of the other and seize all the profits.*

> 77. Experience suggests that this demand of justice can be met in many ways. One of these, and among the most desirable, is to see to it that the workers, in the manner that seems most suitable, are able to participate in the ownership of the enterprise itself. For today more than in the times of Our predecessor *every effort . . . must be made that at least in the future a just share only of the fruits of production be permitted to accumulate in the hands of the wealthy, and that a sufficiently ample share be supplied to the workingmen.*

The Pope says that this just sharing "is a demand of justice" in our day, and a matter of *strict* justice, not a concession by the corporation, since it is more than probable that the worker's labor has gone into the wealth allotted to further productivity and expansion. It is another way in which the Pope sees a more widely diffused ownership of private property in modern society. And while suggestions on how this is to be accomplished are contingent, the concept of co-partnership is not, and, because it is not, it "is a demand of justice."

Since there are many ways of actively sharing in industrial and economic profit, the Pope does not attempt to give specific means of accomplishing this end. The question of profit sharing becomes more complex when it is observed that each industry reinvests a portion of the profits in a renovation of machinery, new construction, expansion of plants, and so on. All this necessary reinvestment is done by the profit which was earned by both industry and labor, and while it is obvious that all of the profit cannot be shared directly, part of the dividends and capital investment can be shared by such means as stocks and bonds. The workers' participation in the actual property of the concern is not merely an act of generosity or efficiency (for instance, a further incentive for more and better production), but desirable in itself as a title of justice (see paragraph 32 for the same idea). In the Pope's mind, the corporation is to become closer to what its name implies: a corporation of both workers and employers who share a mutual responsibility and dignity that proceeds from the ownership of one and same concern. Corporation in this sense is a true and concrete application of what the Pope means by "socialization," one of the main themes of the letter.

Obviously, the ramifications of corporate participation in industry include a great deal more than a "passive" profit sharing which is becoming more common in America. The worker, insists the Pope, must be given a true voice—direct or representative—in the actual management of the industry. For a worker to receive more money is not, strictly speaking, more human; to add a greater human dimension to his role in industry, the worker must accept responsibility, and this can come through an active participation in industrial ownership and management. In paragraphs 91 through 93, the Pope underlines this expanding role for the worker:

91. Following the line of thought of Our predecessors, We defend the desire of employees to participate actively in the management of enterprises in which they are employed. It is not feasible to define a priori the manner and extent of participation of this sort. Such matters must be decided with an eye to specific conditions prevailing in each enterprise. These conditions vary from enterprise to enterprise, and indeed, within the same enterprise frequently undergo sudden and profound changes.

We have no doubt, however, that workers should be allowed to play an active part in the affairs of an enterprise—private or public—in which they are employed. At any rate, every effort should be made that industrial enterprises assume the characteristics of a true human community whose spirit influences the dealings, duties and role of each of its members.

92. This indeed demands that relations between employers and directors on the one hand, and employees on the other, be marked by respect, appreciation, understanding, loyal and active cooperation, and devotion to their common undertaking. It also requires that the work be viewed and

carried out by all the members of the enterprise, not merely as a source of income, but also as the fulfillment of a duty and the performance of a service to others. As a result, the workers should have a timely say in, and be able to make a welcome contribution to, the efficient development of the enterprise.

Our predecessor, Pius XII, remarked that the *economic and social function which every man aspires to fulfill demands that the activity of each be not completely subjected to the will of others.* A humane view of the enterprise ought undoubtedly to safeguard the authority and necessary efficiency associated with unity of direction. It does not follow that those who are daily involved in an enterprise must be reduced to the level of mere silent performers who have no chance to bring their experience into play. They must not be kept entirely passive with regard to the making of decisions that regulate their activity.

93. Finally, attention must be called to the fact that the desire for a greater exercise of serious responsibility on the part of the workers in various productive units corresponds to lawful demands inherent in human nature. It is also in conformity with progressive historical developments in the economic, social and political fields.

The reason for this expanded view of the worker's role mentioned above is that the worker or the professional man perfects himself by and through the work he does. In a very special way, his work expresses his personality, and, as such, it ought to be a true expression of himself. This reflection of the worker's personality in his work cannot be achieved except through responsibility, which in turn cannot be realized without an effective voice in the enterprise in which he works. In his work a man's actions must be those of a free and responsible human being; and for most men, this is almost impossible without an effective sharing in what they do. A man's humanity is expressed in his economic activity, and if this is not free and responsible, his work lacks human dignity. When a man has the opportunity, which is rightfully his, to perfect his human dignity by and through his daily work, his work then represents, in a true sense, a reflection of his person, which is made in the image of God.

This basic insistence on the worker's full sharing in the industrial structure, a tenet that pervades John XXIII's social thought, may seem like a fond dream and not a practical end which is possible to attain. From one viewpoint it is a dream; but to be more accurate, it is an *ideal* that does not now exist. Yet such an ideal can be brought into existence in a society which is truly personalistic and where all forms of private property are open to the use and possession of all individuals. The Pope's personalistic vision of society lies between the total collectivism of socialistic-communism, which merges the individual into a sort of amorphous glob, and the tooth and claw *laissez-faire* capitalism which does not serve the individual from social consideration. In this Christian social order described by Pope John, man becomes more conscious of his freedom and his responsibility, and thus participates more humanly in the economic and political structures to which he belongs.

From this point of view, Americans are at opposite poles in political democracy and social democracy. In the former, each American participates and contributes according to his talents, abilities, and needs. He takes full responsibility as a citizen because political institutions are ultimately directed by him through his representatives. According to *Pacem in terris* (par. 26–27), this political participation is a basic demand of human nature, and corresponds to human dignity because it gives each man a sense of duty and responsibility. Economic society has no such democracy because no responsibility exists for the promotion of human dignity. Insofar as the direction of an enterprise is concerned, the worker is a perpetual minor, a number that can be dismissed or hired according to the "need," determined solely by market demand. His muscle and professional skills are needed, but his opinion and consent are never requested. He is an automaton who is turned on or off. And this view of a man violates all canons of social justice given by the Pope, for the precise reason that an automaton cannot be or develop as a human being. In such a view of man, often assumed by Western capitalism, human dignity and human work are a "commodity to be sold," a cynical view condemned over a hundred years ago by Karl Marx. Until this attitude can be corrected by active participation in industry, the worker's human dignity must remain truncated.

The directives in *Mater et Magistra* are meant to remedy this dehumanizing situation. Though the average American factory worker took home a record $125.00 a week in 1965, his gain in human dignity was not commensurate. To Pope John, an industry or an enterprise is not only a profit making institution, but also a community of persons (par. 93). His understanding of the responsibility of unions to consider the common good (par. 48) and the need for both workers and employers to co-operate in their proper enterprise clearly demonstrate his view of industry as a community:

102. We believe further that one must praise in the same way the outstanding endeavors performed in a true Christian spirit by Our beloved sons in other professional groups and workers' associations which take their inspiration from natural-law principles and show respect for freedom of conscience.

This type of spirit corresponds to the human dignity of workers because it encourages the development of their sense of responsibility toward the industry itself. Yet this end is impossible to achieve without an effective co-partnership, corporation, co-ownership. In Catholic social thought, John XXIII has surpassed all other Popes in his trust and encouragement of the worker in a free society. The ideal social system is not a socialistic, communistic, or capitalistic system; rather it is that system which best promotes human dignity by increasing opportunities for freedom and responsibility in the work to which both worker and employer contribute.

The dignity and personality of the worker are central in paragraphs 82–84 of *Mater et Magistra:*

82. Justice is to be observed not only in the distribution of wealth acquired by production, but also with respect to the conditions under which production is achieved. For there is an innate demand in human nature that when men engage in production they should have the opportunity of exercising responsibility and of perfecting their personalities.

83. It follows that if the organization and operation of an economic system are such as to compromise the human dignity of those who engage in it, or to blunt their sense of responsibility, or to impede the exercise of personal initiative, such an

economic system is unjust. And this is so even if, by hypothesis, the wealth produced through such a system reaches a high level and this wealth is distributed according to standards of justice and equity.

84. It is not possible to describe in detail the sort of economic organization which is more conformed to the dignity of man and more suited to developing his sense of responsibility. Nevertheless, Our predecessor Pius XII opportunely sketches the following directive: *Small and average-sized undertakings in agriculture, in the arts and crafts, in commerce and industry, should be safeguarded and fostered through entry into co-operative unions; in the large concerns, meanwhile, there should be the possibility of modifying the work contract by one of partnership.*

Obviously, a mere multiplication of economic goods or material benefits does not, of itself, enhance human dignity, so both communism and capitalism fall under the same censure when their goals are solely concerned with the material advancement of man. In a sense, East and West suffer from different forms of the same cancer: materialism. According to the Pope, that system alone is moral which permits man free initiative and responsibility in his work. The American system has elevated man's material stature, as the communist system may someday do; yet this does not make them moral or human. A man's dignity is not necessarily increased by the number of autos and gadgets he owns, but also by the intellectual, psychological, and moral fulfillment of his personality through the work which he does. The worker must never be reduced to a passive agent in the production and consumption of goods.

The role of a robot, a cog in a consumptive machine does not correspond to the dignity of man. For the worker, responsibility for production must be added to the consummation of production if America is to attain a human, economic democracy. And since one of the great international threats to American society comes from the destruction of personality by impersonal work on assembly lines, the only way to counteract this uniformity of mass production and mass frustration is for man's participation in society through work to become more human by responsibility. Thus, the insistence of John XXIII on partnership and sharing in enterprise.

The Pope proposes a scale of values which must be observed if a truly human society is to exist. He remarks that this scale is being observed neither in the West nor the East.

> 176. We observe with sadness that many people in the economically advanced countries have no concern for a genuine hierarchy of values. These persons wholly neglect, put aside or flatly deny the existence of spiritual values. Meanwhile they energetically pursue scientific and technological research and seek economic development. Material well-being is in many instances their chief goal in life. This constitutes an insidious poisoning of the aid which economically advanced peoples can give to the underprivileged, in whom ancient tradition has often preserved a living and operative consciousness of the most important values at the base of human culture.

It is unnecessary to belabor the obvious in this statement. Movie stars, baseball players, race track owners are netting fantastic sums of money while millions of the world's people literally starve, even in the United States, where over forty million people are really poor. The spiritual values of which the Pope speaks are those which promote man and make his work in society more humane. We shall later discuss this in relationship to the underdeveloped countries and foreign aid. Thus, the aspect of development of personality is one of the principal factors in the hierarchy of human values, and the Pope's emphasis on labor unions must be seen in this light.

IV

In paragraph 103 of *Mater et Magistra*, Pope John praises the work which has been and is being done by the International Labor Organization of the United Nations, and this praise is well-founded. Because of its concern with poverty, its organization of unions, its education in collective bargaining, its technical assistance, and its training of local technicians, the ILO has helped to alleviate the staggering problems that all the underdeveloped countries of the world must face. And since the despair born of poverty, ignorance, and stagnation is one of the central causes of strained relations among people, the ILO is dedicated to the principle that "lasting peace can be based on social justice" because "poverty anywhere constitutes a danger to prosperity everywhere." Law and order and representative government are important ideals; yet they are empty noises to the starving and hopeless millions. By helping to alleviate these basic material problems, the ILO helps to prepare the way for a meaningful understanding and utilization of these important ideals.

At the 1944 Conference held in Philadelphia, the ILO affirmed the far-reaching and forward looking principles which continue to inspire its programs: "(a) All human beings, irrespective of race, creed, or sex, have the right to pursue both their material well-being and their spiritual development in conditions of freedom and dignity, of economic security and equal opportunity. (b) The attainment of the conditions in which this shall be possible must constitute the central aim of national and international policy."

The following articles of the Universal Declaration of Human Rights which concern labor apply with special force to the ILO, and the ILO has made them its own:

Article 22. Everyone, as a member of society, has the right to social security and is entitled to realization through national effort and international co-operation and in accordance with the organization and resources of each State, of the economic, social and cultural rights indispensable for his dignity and the free development of his personality.

Article 23. Everyone has the right to work, to free choice of employment, to just and favourable conditions of work and to protection against unemployment; everyone, without any discrimination, has the right to equal pay for equal work; everyone who works has the right to just and favourable remuneration ensuring for himself and his family an existence worthy of human dignity, and supplemented, if necessary, by other means of social protection; everyone has the right to form and to join trade unions for the protection of his interests.

Article 24. Everyone has the right to rest and leisure, including reasonable limitation of working hours and periodic holidays with pay.

Article 25. Everyone has the right to a standard

of living adequate for the health and well-being of himself and of his family, including food, clothing, housing and medical care and necessary social services, and the right to security in the event of unemployment, sickness, disability, widowhood, old age or other lack of livelihood in circumstances beyond his control; motherhood and childhood are entitled to special care and assistance; all children, whether born in or out of wedlock, shall enjoy the same social protection.[11]

The Declaration of Human Rights, recognizing the special value of the ILO, lays upon it the solemn obligation to further the following programs among the nations of the world:

(a) Full employment and the raising of standards of living.

(b) The employment of workers in the occupations in which they can have the satisfaction of giving the fullest measure of their skill and attainments and make their greatest contribution to the common well-being.

(c) The provision, as a means of the attainment of this end and under adequate guarantees for all concerned, of facilities for training and the transfer of labour, including migration for employment and settlement.

(d) Policies in regard to wages and earnings, hours and other conditions of work calculated to ensure a just share of the fruits of progress to all, and a minimum living wage to all employed and in need of such protection.

(e) The effective recognition of the right of collective bargaining, the co-operation of

[11] Cf. Pope John's *Pacem in terris*, paragraphs 11, 13, 18, 22–23.

management and labour in the continuous improvement of productive efficiency and the collaboration of workers and employers in the preparation and application of social and economic measures.

(f) The extension of social security measures to provide a basic income to all in need of such protection and comprehensive medical care.

(g) Adequate protection for the life and health of workers in all occupations.

(h) Provisions for child welfare and maternity protection.

(i) The provision of adequate nutrition, housing and facilities for recreation and culture.

One of the greatest accomplishments of the ILO (and the list is long indeed) was the promotion and establishment of a minimum age for those working in industry. Child labor laws were part of its program long before the United States had effective laws against such practices. As early as 1919, the ILO adopted a resolution that no child under fourteen should be employed in industry. In view of the longer period needed to educate the child, the 1937 ILO convention extended this age to fifteen.

The ILO was one of the first voices in the world to advocate universal social security and retirement benefits for the worker when he became too old to care for himself financially. It may seem strange, but little more than a hundred years ago, the lack of old age security was a perpetual fear to working people in all industrialized countries of the world. And it seems almost incredible that the United States, the richest country in the world, had to wait until the 1930's to have this type of national legislation—and a meager one at that. Even today the United States is far behind the ILO's promotion of adequate medical care for the aged. ILO's studies, recommendations, and moral stand on worker welfare were in action long before most Americans even heard of social security and medicare.

The first ILO conference, which meet in 1919, adopted a convention limiting the working hours of persons employed in industry to eight a day and forty-eight a week. Another convention adopted in 1930 extended these limits to workers employed in commerce and offices. The next important step came in 1935 with the adoption of the forty-hour-week convention. Member states of the ILO were requested to approve the principle of the forty-hour week in such a way that the worker's standard of living would not be reduced.

Another important program of the ILO which it still continues to pursue is equal pay for equal work done by women. As the Pope points out in *Pacem in terris* (par. 41), women are beginning to take their places along with men in the world of culture and work. The ILO has been promoting the principle of worker equality among men and women, without destroying women's special position within the family. Male and female equality in work was one of the principal features of the ILO's Equal Remuneration Convention of 1951. (In the United States such national legislation was finally passed in 1964.) Thus, the main function of the ILO is to act as a pace-setter, and, through its activities, participating national governments can measure their progress toward social justice.

These activities are by no means the only constructive endeavors of the ILO. This organization acts as a clearing house for information and advice on training, labor-management relations, union organization and collective bargaining. Conferences held in various parts of the world give direction and impetus to ILO programs in the regions for which they are destined. ILO operational activities began on a large scale in 1950 with the inception of the United Nations Expanded Program for Technical Assistance (EPTA). Since that time, more than 1100 ILO experts have been sent on technical co-operation missions to over 86 countries and territories. Over 1,500 fellowships have been granted to promising nations in the effort to improve specialized knowledge and foreign study. The ILO also provides technical assistance under four separate programs: EPTA, the Special Fund, ILO Regular Budget Program, and Funds in Trust. Under this wide sweep of programs (over forty million dollars' worth) more than 80 countries receive desperately needed technical assistance and aid.

It is no wonder that the Pope explicitly praises the efforts and programs of the ILO in his *Mater et Magistra.*

CHAPTER THREE

Private Property

I

IN RECENT YEARS, expanded notions of the concept of private property have developed, and from a dynamically comprehensive point of view, Pope John proceeds to adjust these new developments to the traditional concept of private property. Among these new developments are the changes which have occurred in industrial management, ownership of capital goods, professional ability and competence, and the creation of various types of sickness and old-age insurances which have replaced patrimonies as the source of security for old age and survivors. These and other modern developments have modified the use of private property in the workaday life of many citizens, and, in effect, modern society now faces a new situation. But though this new condition of modern society modifies the traditional concept, the right of individual citizens to own and administer private property is not destroyed.[1]

To understand Pope John's reconsideration of the concept of private property, it must be made clear that the right of usage is prior to and conditions the right to private property. God has created man as a body and a soul, an incarnate being, and, as such, man has a natural right to use the world's goods for the conservation of his

[1] See *Mater et Magistra,* paragraphs 43, 104–121.

life, the fruition of his talents, and the protection of his health. This right precedes the right of property, and, in traditional Catholic social thought, the right to property is a derivative, or a concretization, of the right of usage. In other words, the right to use material goods is fundamental and primary, while the right to own material goods is secondary and derived. The right to property exists so that an order might be established by which the right of usage is assured and guaranteed.

The right of property is a means to an end, and it is therefore subordinate to the right of usage, the end itself. Since every means is relative, the doctrine of the *absolute* right of private property is a grave social aberration. Clearly, then, private property must ultimately promote the right of usage. For example, large land holdings in the hands of a few Latin Americans is a serious disorder because the right of usage is denied to the many. To correct this disorder, agrarian reform is a pressing need of social justice in many of these Latin American countries.[2] Property is thus a social responsibility, and it must be used to promote the general welfare. The social responsibility which accrues to the right of private property is a fundamental concept in the social thought of recent popes.

> 43. Concerning the use of material goods, Our predecessor declares that the right of every man to use them for his subsistence is prior to all other rights of an economic nature, even to the right of private property. Undoubtedly, adds Our predecessor, the right of private property is also a natural right. Nevertheless, in the objective order established by God, this right should be so arranged that

---

[2] J. B. Gremillion, "The Challenge of International Justice" in *The Christian Challenge in Latin America* (Maryknoll, N. Y., 1964), p. 16.

it does not hinder the satisfaction of *the unquestionable need that goods, which God created for all men, should flow equitably to all, according to the principles of justice and charity.*

This paragraph is a clear development of the idea in Pius XII's radio message of 1941. In this message Pius XII stated:

> Every man, as a living being gifted with reason, has in fact from nature the fundamental right to make use of the material goods of the earth, while it is left to the will of man . . . to regulate in greater detail the actuation of this right. This individual right cannot in any way be suppressed, even by other clear and undisputed rights over material goods; undoubtedly, the natural order, deriving from God, demands also private property . . . But all this remains subordinate to the natural scope of material goods and cannot emancipate itself from the first and fundamental right which concedes their use to all men.[5]

The words of Pius XII are clear, and Pope John simply makes them his own. This concept of the right of usage is further emphasized in *Pacem in terris:*

> 21. The right to private property, even of productive goods, also derives from the nature of man. This right, as We have elsewhere declared, is *an effective aid in safeguarding the dignity of the human person and the free exercise of responsibility in all fields of endeavor. Finally, it strengthens the stability and tranquility of family life, thus*

[5] Pius XII on the anniversary of *Rerum Novarum* in *The Major Addresses of Pius XII,* I (St. Paul, 1961), pp. 30–31.

contributing to the peace and prosperity of the commonwealth.

22. However, it is opportune to point out that there is a social duty essentially inherent in the right of private property.

This principle of social philosophy allows for such necessities in modern social life as agrarian reform, the nationalization of basic industries in case of true public need, the right of eminent domain, and civil rights legislation which demands equal public accommodation for all citizens.

In this distinction between the right of usage and the right to private property, recent popes are merely observing the traditional teaching of the Church. St. Thomas developed the distinction between *jus proprietatis* and *jus utendi* as early as 1260. In the *Summa Theologica,* he argues that private property is not a primary right, but a derived and secondary right.[4] The material goods of this earth are common to all men and they are destined by their nature for the use of all men. The right of private property, however, is a secondary right that is derived from the right of usage in order to make it concrete and specific.[5] Furthermore, St. Thomas called the possession of property "common" in the sense that it is to be used responsibly for the needs and necessities of all men.[6] Pope John maintains the same doctrine concerning the common destiny of the material goods of this earth:

19. The right to own private property, including productive goods, is a natural one, which the state cannot suppress. Embedded in its nature is a social

[4] II-II, q. 57, a. 2 and 3
[5] I-II, q. 94, a. 5.
[6] II-II, q. 66, a. 21; also II-II, q. 65 a. 1 and 7.

function; on this account it is a right to be exercised both for one's personal benefit and for the good of others.[7]

The teaching of the Pope is traditional, for it was precisely for this reason that the famous "right of the poor" was staunchly defended by the writers of the Middle Ages. When material goods become a pressing need for a man to live, their "common" possession allows him the right to take what he needs in spite of all human conventions or laws of property. This principle was practiced only in cases of true emergency, but the principle is a good one and clearly shows the relative character of private property as a means to an end. *In necessitate, omnia sunt communia* ("In necessity, all things are common"). The Pope will apply this aspect of the right of usage on an international scale: the rich nations have an obligation in strict justice to aid economically underdeveloped countries. We shall treat this in a later chapter.

Since the right of usage is primary in character, it ranks among the fundamental rights of man. Only within its context can the concept of the right to private property be developed. The idea that private property is an absolute right, preached by nineteenth-century *laissez-faire* liberalism and persisting into the twentieth-century, is immoral and a "grave aberration" of social justice. Since it is a means, private property must always remain subordinate to its proper end, the right of usage. And although private property is not at the service of the state, it does have a social function and responsibility; it is at the service of man. Private property must always and everywhere be used to promote the dignity and personality of all men. When abuses of the right to

[7] The Latin is very strong here. After "nature" we have *"verum,"* which cannot be translated into English. It is a word of strong emphasis. Cf. par. 30, 119 and 120 as well.

private property occur, they must be firmly corrected by the state in order to prevent the development of an inhuman social order. Government's duty to promote the right of usage justifies the objectives of legislation such as Title II of the Civil Rights Bill of 1964, which deals with public accommodations. In defending discriminatory housing laws by such means as the repeal of the California Rumford Act, various real estate groups violate all the canons of social justice under the pretense of promoting the right to private property.

All of these considerations on the right of usage do not change or supplant the natural right to own private property, though some persons have made such a conclusion after a rapid reading of the encyclical. A closer examination, however, will show that this interpretation is not correct. On the contrary the right to private property is more important today than ever before, and though Pope John wants to expand the concept of private property to include recent developments, his argument rests solely on traditional thought. In short, the Pope wants to show that private property is a relative right and not absolute as the nineteenth-century Manchesterian liberals maintained.

The Pope's argument to expand the concept of private property comes out of his keen understanding of the new conditions in modern economic society. Until comparatively recent times, most people lived on farms. To most farmers, the normal means to security was a patrimony of stable capital goods which could be depended upon to provide food and shelter. Today, a man provides security for himself and his family through such things as health, survivor, and old-age insurance.

105. It is also true that there are many citizens today—and their number is on the increase—who,

through belonging to insurance groups or through social security, have reason to face the future with serenity. Formerly such serenity depended on the ownership of properties, however modest.

Above all, however, a man today no longer makes his livelihood by his work on a farm; he does so by virtue of his professional skill. Over 80% of the people in modern Western society live in metropolitan areas and derive their livelihood directly from their professional skills. This demand for professional skill is becoming so prevalent that in the next five to ten years, students without technical training, or "drop-outs," will have no possibility of finding work.[8]

106. Finally, it is noted that today men strive to acquire professional skills rather than to become owners of property. They have greater confidence in income derived from work or rights founded on work than in income derived from capital or rights founded on capital.

107. Moreover, this is in conformity with the superior nature of work since it is the immediate product of a human person. Capital, on the contrary, must be regarded as by its nature merely an instrument. Such a view of work may no doubt be considered a step forward in the process of human civilization.

The dependency on one's knowledge and skills is more human than the dependency on land and capital. In the former, man develops himself through what is most intimate—his own talents and abilities; in the latter, he develops himself through a concern with inanimate and exterior objects. Work is noble, a further-

[8] S. Lichter *et al.*, *The Drop-outs* (New York, 1962), pp. 3–7.

ing of God's creative act, and it is the means of bringing about the objects which men need for the development of their interior values. By depending more on his work for security, man is acting more in conformity with his human dignity, because the responsibility for what he does and why he does it touches his interior life.

This shift from dependence on capital goods to professional skills is an important effect of socialization (see Pope John's discussion in par. 59–62) and, as such, is to be considered a step forward. By its very nature, socialization has been both the cause and the effect of the complexity and the enrichment of our modern civilization, and since the process of socialization has been intensified through the increasing interrelationships of professional and technical skills, these skills must now be an integral part of any consideration of modern civilization. Through these complex interrelationships, the objective culture of mankind has been enriched: that is, the objective elements such as art, architecture, painting, writing, technology, and so on, which are realized by human labor and which transform the world.

In its turn the objective culture has enriched the subjective culture of humanity; that is, each person in a society perfects himself scientifically, intellectually, culturally, morally, and in every way possible, limited only by his will and abilities.[9] This enrichment has been brought about through the specialization in professional and technical skills by an ever-increasing number of people in modern society. Their dependency is no longer on a patrimony of capital goods, but on these acquired professional abilities. The Pope considers this form of security a better expression of the human per-

[9] See the development of this whole theme in *Pacem in terris,* par. 18–22, Riga, *op. cit.,* pp. 54–55.

71

sonality, and these abilities and the social security which comes out of them must now rank in equal importance with the traditional patrimony of private property.

In a consideration of socialization and the effect that professional and technical skills have had upon it, the Pope's observations and approval of group insurances known as social security deserve special attention. Before 1935, such programs were not available in the United States; so that here, at least, a concern with this aspect of modern life is recent. Left in the flux of capitalistic liberalism's dog-eat-dog system, which finally collapsed in 1929, the dignity of the human person suffered severe blows. Since modern man's dignity grows out of his professional skills rather than his capital goods, the material basis needed to protect his dignity must be provided in new ways. Recent systems of social security are good means to provide this material basis for human dignity, and they are certainly in conformity with man's basic right to dignity and economic independence. Because they are proper means to the end, they are approved by Pope John:

> 136. Systems of social insurance and social security can contribute effectively to the redistribution of national income according to standards of justice and equity. These systems can therefore be looked on as instruments for restoring balance between standards of living among different categories of the population.

The "different categories of the population" must include the sick, the aged, and the widowed, who traditionally have had very low incomes and who, even today, are in the lowest income brackets. During inflationary times, these limited incomes are depressed even further. Obviously, it is morally incumbent on public and private authorities to re-adjust the level of income for these people in such times. Nor is it beyond the demands of social justice for pensioners in some way to share in the increased profits of their former employees. As constituted today, corporations distribute all profits to shareholders alone, who take minimum risks but are entitled to huge profits. In the first half of 1964, for example, General Motors had a net profit of 30% (1.5 billion dollars). Justice certainly demands that part of this profit be redistributed to pensioners whose labor and toil was also responsible for this progress.

Medical insurance for the aged is another aspect of social security which fulfills the demands of social justice. Among all Catholic thinkers on social problems, it is an established canon that each person has a right to all necessary medical care, whether or not he can afford it. The application of this principle will vary from country to country because of the variance in economic and social well-being, but to deny the validity of the principle is to desert the individual human being to the brutal uncertainties of chance.[10] While the rich do not suffer from a denial of equal medical care, the poor are punished; and while the inhumanity of such a denial is evident, the vicious irony that it engenders comes out of a punishment imposed for the crime of poverty. As Pope John put it, "Every man has the right to life, to bodily integrity, and to means which are necessary and suitable for the proper development of life. These are primarily food, clothing, shelter, rest, medical care and finally the necessary social services. Therefore, a human being also has the right to security in case of sickness . . ." (*Pacem in terris*, par. 11).

The Pope gives no specific plan to insure medical

[10] Masse, *op. cit.*, pp. 119–120.

care, for this would be outside the competence of papal social teaching. Yet the principle and its concomitants are very clear: every man has a right to proper medical care, and if he cannot afford the medical care he needs, the state has an obligation to assist him. For many in the younger age groups, such security is amply assured by private plans such as Blue Cross and Blue Shield. Many professions add medical insurance as a "fringe benefit" for both the employee and his entire family. Unfortunately, there are two categories of people in our society who cannot afford such insurance: the poor and the aged. Since the problems of the poor have already been discussed, here it is only necessary to add that some type of assistance must be rendered to them, particularly in the slums. The poor are sick more often and for longer periods of time than the rich or middle classes. The reason is not hard to find: their food is inferior, and preventive medicine non-existent. In the slums and for the poor, government supported clinics must be provided, at least until better ways can be made practical.

A more topical problem in medical insurance is that of the aged who live on limited incomes. The aged are sick more often and for much longer periods of time than younger people, and sickness comes to them precisely at a time when they can least afford it. Private insurances refuse to accept them because they are "high risks," or if they do, the premiums are so high that few of the 19 million people over age 65 in the United States can afford them. For the most part, consequently, they are chronically ill from a want of the most elementary preventive or corrective medicine. They never go to a doctor until they must be rushed to a hospital, and by this time, physical and mental damage has been done. Those who deny these realities ought to live with the aged for a while to see the truth of this monstrous condition.

The argument that the aged should have saved for such an eventuality is totally false for at least two reasons. Given the great cost of medical and hospital care today, any major disease can be financially disastrous, even for the family that has a moderate income but is not protected by some form of medical insurance. This is doubly true for the aged whose meager savings and income could not begin to meet the probable eventualities of old age. Second, the aged are poor, not because they did not save, but because they could not save. To bring up children, they barely made ends meet during their working years. And since the real affluence in American society did not begin until the 1950's, the working years of today's old people were not remunerative enough for systematic saving. They prepared the seed-bed for the present affluent generation by their labors, and it is only just that the new society share the harvest. In the United States the demand is evident, for this is the only country in the Western world which lacks some type of old-age medical insurance financed through social security.[10b] Since the United States is the richest country in the world, Europeans are struck by the American attitude toward the aged, and many of them think it downright cruel and selfish.

To a degree, this European judgment is true. A recent study by the Senate subcommittee on the health of the elderly shows the pathetic plight of the aged. The study focused on the number of older persons covered by health insurance, on the adequacy of the policies, and on the cost of the premiums. The subcommittee reported that only 9 million older Americans, half of

[10b] A mild Medicare Bill for the aged was passed by Congress in 1965.

those who are 65 years of age or older, held any kind of private health insurance at the end of 1962. Because the better commercial health insurance plans are so expensive, they are beyond the economic reach of most older persons. In fact, only one in four older persons enjoys adequate hospital insurance under the definition of adequacy established by the American Hospital Association (this yardstick calls for a policy whose benefits pay at least 75% of all hospital costs). On the other hand, more than half of all commercial policies held by elderly persons pay $10 a day or less toward hospital charges for room and board, which currently average about $27 a day. The subcommittee also reported that the 9 million older Americans without any private health insurance are "predominately the very old, those in poor health, and unemployed and those with the lowest incomes." These, the subcommittee said, are the ones who need protection the most. As a check to public apathy, the subcommittee disputed the claim made by private health insurance spokesmen that 10.3 million older Americans now had health insurance. "The subcommittee is convinced that this is an inflated figure, concocted to create an illusion of great strides by private health insurance in extending coverage to the aged. . . . In reality, the 'stride' was no more than a 'limp.' "

Other reports and studies show the same desperate plight of the aged. The Senate report of 1960 stated that "at least one half of the aged—approximately eight million people—cannot afford today decent housing, proper nutrition, adequate medical care, preventive or acute, or necessary recreation." The same judgment was made in 1961 by the White House Conference on Aging: "Many states report that half their citizens over 65 have incomes too low to meet their basic needs."

Over half of these people are covered by some kind of Federal program (social security, old-age assistance, and so on). Yet, the social security payments are, by Federal admission, completely inadequate to a decent life. In 1959, for instance, they averaged a little better than $70 a month. Or, to take another expression of the same fact, the senate report concluded that if aged couples could live within the low cost minimum food budget of the Department of Agriculture, a quarter of them would be spending more than half their income on food alone.[11]

The average American family spends less than 20% of its income on food. These statistics lend credence to the European view that American society is obsessed by youth and frightened by age and death—so frightened, perhaps, that in avoiding all thoughts of age and death, Americans do an injustice to the aged by neglecting their problems.

In 1964, Congress took a step in the right direction by increasing social security benefits by 5%, but this is not enough. The reality of poverty among millions of American old people suggests that the government alone is capable of dealing with the problem. The American government has declared a war on poverty, and it is reasonable that a new front be opened in the area of poverty among the aged. Medical insurance under social security, for example, could help alleviate such poverty by providing medical care for the aged that every human being has a right to receive.

To conclude, then, all of these specific programs that provide adequate health, education, and welfare for citizens who have not sought security through the tradi-

[11] M. Harrington, *The Other America* (New York, 1962), pp. 104–105.

tional patrimony, but have developed professional and technical skills, are symptoms of a new conception of life. In this new conception, capital and private property still remain an important means to human security, but these new, and perhaps more humane, sources of security must also be regarded as legitimate and welcome. Private property is not only security, but an expression of human personality, and only insofar as it remains a means to this end can it be defended as a fulfillment of human aspirations. Corresponding to this means of human fulfillment, however, is the security provided by public insurance; but above all, the aspirations of most contemporary men are fulfilled by the skills and abilities through which they earn their daily bread. And since modern man accepts the responsibility of his work, which enhances his dignity, his work cannot be subservient to private property without demeaning his humanity. Understanding this drift of the modern era, Pope John recognizes that professional skill and social security have modified, but not abolished, the traditional concept of private property.

This paragraph is a clear development of the idea in Pius XII's radio message of 1941. In this message, he stated:

> Every man, as a living being gifted with reason, has in fact from nature the fundamental right to make use of the material goods of the earth, while it is left to the will of man . . . to regulate in greater detail the actuation of this right. This individual right cannot in any way be suppressed, even by other clear and undisputed rights over material goods; undoubtedly, the natural order, deriving from God, demands also private property . . . But all this remains subordinate to the natural scope of mate-

rial goods and cannot emancipate itself from the first and fundamental right which concedes their use to all men.[12]

II

In *Mater et Magistra* the right to private property is not only subordinate to the right of usage of the world's goods, but as a concrete application of this principle, it can never be held superior to a man's right to life and the corresponding means necessary to insure that right. This right, to be efficacious and vital, must be underpinned by solid guarantees of a minimum subsistence for the life of a man and his family. Pope John summed this up in *Pacem in terris* when he said, "Each man has a right to life, to bodily integrity and to the means which are necessary and suitable for the proper development of life; these are primarily food, clothing, shelter, rest, medical care and finally the necessary social services" (par. 11). Since this paragraph comes before any discussion of private property (e.g., par. 21), the conclusion to be drawn is that in the hierarchy of values, guarantees for an effective right to life such as social security, old-age pensions, unemployment insurance, and plans for proper medical aid are primary and, as such, they better express the modern world's need for security than does the institution of private property in its traditional forms. This modern development of social securities corresponds to the present condition of socialization and acts as an effective guarantee of the right to life and the "common destiny of this world's goods."[13]

Yet, the right of private property remains unchanged even though these new developments cannot be disregarded. In the words of the Pope:

[12] Pius XII on the Anniversary of Rerum Novarum in *The Major Addresses of Pius XII*, I (St. Paul, 1961), pp. 30–31.
[13] P. Haubtman, *l'Eglise Mère et Educatrice* (Paris, 1964), p. 193.

111. Accordingly, We make Our own the insistence of Our predecessor Pius XII: *In defending the principle of private property the Church is striving after an important ethico-social goal. She does not intend solely and merely to uphold the present state of affairs as if it were an expression of the Divine Will to protect on principle the rich and plutocrats against the poor and indigent. . . . The Church rather aims at seeing to it that the institution of private property is such as it should be according to the plan of Divine Wisdom and the disposition of nature.* And thus this natural right ought to be both the guarantee of the essential freedom of the individual and an indispensable element in the structuring of a sound social order.

The essential reason for this right is always the same: it permits the expansion of the human personality in the pursuit of a stable and concrete good. The error of the nineteenth century (and to a lesser degree in our day) was that the right to private property was believed absolute. When arguments are adduced to defend its absolute character, the arguments, in reality, either defend the *status quo* of the powerful and rich (the capitalists in the nineteenth-century or the Latin American land-lords in the twentieth) or perpetuate an evil social system which has failed to acknowledge the social responsibilities of private property (opposition to the public accommodation clause of the new Civil Rights Bill). The popes, however, insist on the social character of private property, and do so in order to assure that, always and everywhere, it will serve to help fulfill the personalities of all citizens in every community.

Pope John's observation that private property is a

guarantee of human freedom clearly corroborates his predecessors' basic view. Since it is dangerous for a man to remain totally dependent on the contemporary state which is characterized by impersonality and complex socialization, private property acts as a buffer to the all-consuming power the state can have over the individual. Through private property, man can initiate his personal development and provide for his own security; and without it, "the fundamental manifestations of freedom are suppressed or stifled" (par. 109). Private property is thus an unambiguous manifestation of the individual's priority over the state, and since the individual is always prior to the state by natural law, any truly free society cannot and will not unnecessarily restrict this right.

Without a right to private property, in the form either of capital goods or of securities, man is reduced to economic and personal slavery. To lack freedom does not necessarily mean that a man must be confined in a jail; slavery is also that condition in which a man has no security for the future, and in such a condition, he cannot live in peace of mind. The Pope stresses this guarantee of freedom which comes with the right to various forms of private property:

> 109. There is no reason for such a doubt to persist. The right of private ownership of goods, including productive goods, has a permanent validity. This is so because it is a part of the natural law, which teaches us that individuals are prior to society and that society has as its purpose the service of man.
>
> Moreover, it would be useless to insist on free, private initiative in the economic field, if the same initiative does not include the power to dispose

freely of the means indispensable to its exercise. Further, history and experience testify that where governments fail to recognize private ownership of goods, productive goods included, the fundamental manifestations of freedom are suppressed or stifled. Hence one may justifiably conclude that the exercise of freedom finds both a guarantee and an incentive in the right of ownership.

The Pope's discussion of private property follows his analysis of other forms of security in our day, and since both conform to man's nature, both forms of security must now be considered in any understanding of social justice. It is no longer possible to say that the regime of private property as traditionally expressed is *the* ideal towards which society must evolve. *De facto,* society has evolved differently and the Pope notes and approves this evolution: social security and public insurances are not necessarily worth less or less desirable than private property, and vice versa.

The Pope's view of private property represents a forward movement in making human the socialization which is one of the characteristic features of our civilization. Work is the expression of man himself, while inert capital is but an instrument of man's security. The middle-sized or larger corporations always remain private property, but, as explained, the Pope prefers them jointly owned by workers and employers, since it is the work of both which has been responsible for growth and production. Both should share and own what they commonly toil to build and perfect. This does not, however, eliminate the possibility that the state can, in cases of the common good, own and nationalize basic economic industries.

116. The doctrine that has been set forth above

obviously does not prohibit the state and other public agencies from lawfully possessing productive goods, particularly when they *carry with them an opportunity for domination that is so great that it cannot be left in the hands of private individuals without injury to the community at large.*

Such projects need not be totally owned and operated by public authorities. To the degree possible, joint participation by public, private, and even citizen groups is feasible in projects such as TVA, power and irrigation developments, land reclamation, scientific research, communication satellites, and so on. To accuse public authorities of unwarranted interference with private initiative in these spheres is short-sighted and unjust, especially when one considers that the initial capital investment for the development of things like TVA and missiology was public tax monies. The taxpayer has a right to expect some kind of return on the enormous sums of money spent on programs for the public good.

The public ownership of industry has been hotly contested, and its adoption gives rise to considerations of great social importance. The central problem, of course, is whether its adoption sounds the death knell for private property and gives victory to those who have opposed it as unjust. The Pope believes this is not the case:

. . . until recently some movements which have for their purpose the reconciliation of justice and liberty in society were clearly opposed to private ownership of productive goods; but now, being more fully enlightened concerning actual social conditions, they have modified their stand and are taking an essentially positive attitude toward that right. (Par. 110.)

Many social movements in the past were opposed to the private ownership of the chief industries: such ownership in the hands of a few gave great power to be used as an instrument of oppression. Moreover, various socialistic groups saw that economic individualism, particularly that of the nineteenth-century, gave rise to deep class antagonisms. To a great degree, these conditions have been changed; economic power and private property are no longer the same thing. They no longer coincide. Material property and the power it engenders have been artificially separated, and the direct ownership of capital goods is of less importance today than their effective management and control. In fact, property ownership is no longer necessary for the effective distribution of wealth. Many so-called socialistic parties —especially of the English type—do not specifically attack the institution of private property, though they do attack its abuse and maldistribution.[14]

Though many of the socialist-type groups have not denied the right to private property, they have claimed that its effective use in society, at least in the larger and more powerful industries, could not be administered by private owners without abuse. There is much truth in this accusation as any cursory glance at nineteenth-century economic history will disclose. The solution proposed by these groups was and is nationalization. The Pope, however, is cautious in accepting this.

117. In modern times there is an evident tendency toward a progressive transfer to property to

[14] G. Purnell, "Socialism and the Encyclicals" in *Blackfriars,* 45 (April, 1964), p. 173.

the state or other agencies of public law. The explanation of this tendency is to be found in the ever-widening activity which the common good requires that public authorities undertake. But even in this eventuality the principle of subsidiarity stated above is to be faithfully observed. Accord-ingly, the state and other agencies of public law should not extend their ownership except where evident and real needs of the common good dictate it. And they should be on guard against extending it to the point where private property is excessively reduced or, even worse, abolished.

Yet, nationalization is not denied as a possible means to social justice.[15] In case of true necessity, the state can nationalize various industries for the public good (par. 116). The Church certainly teaches that Marxism or any doctrine which denies man's natural right to private property is a grave danger to the freedom of man in society; yet the Church also teaches that the abusive use of private property by a small group of capitalists can also be as grave a danger to society.

Everyone, teaches the Church, has the right to own private goods for the security and expansion of his personality. This right comes from God and cannot be denied in principle since man has need of these goods to live a full and human life. Under the Pope's concept, private property can take the form of productive goods, consumer goods (or the money with which to buy them), securities, or professional abilities. These prod-ucts and abilities are necessary if man is to gain his livelihood in a personal, responsible, and dignified way. But the right to private property does not exclude the possibility that serious economic problems may force

[15] See Pius XII's talk, 14 September, 1952; *AAS*, 44 (1952), p. 297.

the government of a country to take a more active part in the planning and administration of the economy. Since the instruments of production are at the disposition of man for the expansion of his personality and since the economic order will vary in each country, each concrete situation must be closely examined to determine the extent to which state intervention is necessary and proper. In the United States, given rapid and radical economic changes such as automation, industrial capacity, and international trade balances, the need for planning by industry, labor, and government becomes more evident every day. In our time of ever-growing socialization, it is strange to hear people defend the traditional concept of an unrestricted market as the principal, if not the only, determinant of the economy. This attitude is the residue of *laissez-faire* economic thinking, and no one who wishes full employment and a more equitable distribution of wealth can take it seriously. Economic planning is an obvious necessity for economic growth to proceed at a healthy rate.

In paragraph 113, the Pope insists that "it is not enough to assert the natural character of the right of private property, including productive property; strenuous efforts also must be made to see that the ability to exercise this right is extended to all social classes." The essential purpose of economic planning or of any economic system must be to facilitate man's accessibility to the goods which he needs to conduct a dignified and human life. Among these necessary goods are included housing, sufficient and varied foods, insurances and securities for old age, for sickness and for survivors, and other durable goods which a man needs to develop his higher facilities, such as transportation, books, radios, and TV, but these latter will depend upon the degree of development in any particular economy. In the United

States, these durable goods are a necessity for the type of civilization which exists, and that is why the "war on poverty" is a just objective of the American government. To obtain these durable goods, the help of the government is often necessary in such projects as urban renewal, mass transportation, and cheap power for agricultural regions (TVA). A clear distinction must be made, however, between the ownership of these goods and of the capitalistic productive goods. Publicly owned goods do not fall under the same categorical imperatives as do privately owned goods. Publicly owned goods may be, and usually have been, conducive to a better distribution of wealth, of production, of industry, but they need not be. They may simply exist for the public good. And while the capitalistic system of free enterprise as developed in the United States conditions our thinking toward the development of property, it is not part of the natural law, and its processes must not be construed as part of the moral order. Its continuation or discontinuation must be judged on only one criterion: Does it or does it not lead to a personal economic expansion of American citizens which is in keeping with the demands of human nature?

To summarize, the teaching of the Church on the question of private property has many nuances. While the Church recognizes that the right to private property is a natural right, she also recognizes that the right is not absolute. Goods are always means to accomplish a certain end, and their development and distribution can be conditioned by and accommodated to various economic systems. In all systems, however, the essential purpose of private property must be to further the development of the personality of men. All men must have access to the basic, durable goods in a society, and when any group of men do not have this access, then the public authorities should correct this injustice. In this age of abundance, when our industrial and technical capacity is prolifically active, it is intolerable that some 35 million Americans live in poverty.

In recommending economic systems, however, the Church is very prudent. She has no doctrinaire preference for any particular system, neither capitalism nor socialism. While the principle of subsidiarity is always valid, she is fully aware that societies as well as economies differ, and she leaves the practical implementation of the principles of social justice to each particular country. Time and circumstances change: what is good today may not be good tomorrow, and what is good for the American economy might not be good for that of Indonesia. The principles do not change, but a host of specific conditions such as the degree of industrial development, underdeveloped mineral resources, retarded areas of the economy, and pockets of poverty may exist in one country and not another. The existence of such conditions, however, is not to be used as an excuse for the *status quo,* as in certain countries in Latin and Central America. The right of property implies an *effective* guarantee to all men of at least some durable goods.

115. Today more than ever the wider distribution of private ownership ought to be forcefully championed. As We have noted, the economies of an increasing number of nations are in the process of rapid development. Making wise use of proven techniques, these communities will not find it difficult to adjust their socio-economic order in such a way as to facilitate the widest possible spread of private ownership in goods of this sort: durable consumer goods, housing, farms, one's own

equipment in artisan enterprises and family-type farms, shares in middle-sized and large corporations. Such a policy has already been tried with success in some nations that have more advanced economic and social systems.

The *latifundias* can find no justification here, nor can the American Catholic who knows, even if he cannot see, that millions of his fellow Americans do not share in the abundance of America—*a fortiori*, the millions of the world's poor. The goods of a particular society must be effectively distributed to all the classes of its citizens. The essential point is that each man in any society ought to have enough durable and productive goods to insure his initiative, autonomy, security, and, consequently, his individual responsibility and dignity.

III

Moving his discussion to the public authority, the Holy Father reminds public servants that they must be competent in their particular fields:

> 118. Nor is one to forget that the economic activities of the state and other agencies of public law are to be entrusted to those who embody exceptional ability, tested probity and a keen sense of responsibility toward their country. Further, their behavior ought to be subject to sound and constant inspection in order to prevent the concentration of economic power in the hands of a few within the state's own organization. This would evidently conflict with the highest purpose of the state.

But technical ability is not the only qualification necessary in a public servant.[16] Authority is a service

[16] See *Pacem in terris*, par. 46–54.

and a love; so the man with authority must serve the public by directing it to a proper end, which is the common good, with a love for the persons he must direct. Since the end determines the competence and limits of authority, the persons who are to attain this end determine the amount of authority which must be used. Yet persons under authority must act on their own initiative. Authority, then, must never crush this personal initiative, because it is always at the service of this initiative. It must respect the initiative of others; it must supplement initiative when necessary; it must orientate initiative when it deviates from the right course; and it can use force if necessary, but only as a last resort. Authority is not defined by force or the ability to apply superior violence;[17] it is defined as a means directed toward the common good of its citizens, which is the end to be pursued in justice and love. In contrast to this concept of authority, the notion of authority as an end, or organized society as an end (modern totalitarianisms and nationalism), or of the absolute value of private property as an end (nineteenth-century Manchesterian liberalism) are all destructive of the human goals of justice, of responsibility, and, ultimately, of peace in the community.

To the extent that they directly or indirectly make material betterment the highest form of human achievement, modern Western democracies also use authority for wrong ends. Contrary to Christian tradition, the West is beginning to have a great deal in common with the communist world. On each side of the Iron Curtain, a deeply disturbing variety of the same moral sickness festers: both sides root their view of life in the same type of materialism. Both sides are basically opportunistic and pragmatic. More serious, however, is that on the

---

[17] C. Frankel, *The Case for Modern Man* (Boston, 1959), p. 30.

moral level, both sides are blindly passive in their submission to a type of atomic determinism which, in effect, leaves men completely irresponsible. Whatever else may be said about the nuclear arms race, one thing is certain: rationality is ebbing away, and threats and counterthreats on both sides of the Iron Curtain allow the reign of irrationality.

Karl Barth has warned the West of this impending loss of moral distinction. Barth argues that Nazism attempted to defeat the Church by perverting its doctrines with cultural heresies; communism, however, is an atheistic political system based upon philosophical ideals that must be countered with other ideals. But God, Barth notes, is not an idea, not a banner for human concepts and intentions. Yet many people believe that Christianity is a kind of moral, religious, and political idea which confronts this atheistic idea of communism. To Barth, the capitalistic West is as materialistic as the communistic East, and, being so, it represents a serious temptation to the Church, since the West tries to cloak its political ambition and basic materialistic intentions in moral terms. The Popes themselves have made this observation many times in their social teachings. As recently as June of 1964, Pope Paul VI posed this very problem to members of the Christian Union of Businessmen and Executives:

The business enterprise, which by its nature demands collaboration, accord, harmony, is it still not today a clash of minds and of interests? And sometimes is it not considered an indictment of the one who puts it together, directs it and administers it? Is it not said of you that you are the capitalists and the only guilty ones? Are you not often the target of social dialectic? There must be something profoundly mistaken, something radically lacking in the system itself, if it gives rise to such social reactions. It is true that whoever speaks of capitalism today, as many do, with the concepts that defined it in the past century, gives proof of being out of touch with reality. But it remains a fact that the socio-economic system generated from Manchesterian Liberalism still persists. It persists in the connection of the one-sidedness of possession of the means of production and of the economy directed toward private profit . . . Such an outlook [materialism] is attributable not only to those who make the fundamental dogma of their unhappy sociology out of an antique dialectic materialism [Marxism], but also to the many who erect a golden calf in the place belonging to the God of heaven and earth![18]

Christians must make a judgment on both sides of the Iron Curtain, and the sole criterion must be the Church's social teaching.

IV

When Pope John speaks about the natural right to private property, including productive or capital goods, he does not mean to oppose this to socialized forms of ownership. Some people have derived this conclusion from a cursory reading of *Mater et Magistra*, but a fuller reading of the letter will reveal that the Pope, speaking for the Church, approves the fact that ownership can accrue to private individuals or to some form of employee-employer combination (a socialized form of ownership). Since the socialized forms of ownership have already been discussed at some length, it is not

[18] Reported in *The Catholic Messenger*, 82 (June 18, 1964), p. 9.

necessary to return to them here.[19] Since public ownership comes under this heading, a few words of justification are in order. The public ownership of industries is
permissible and proper when they become truly vital to
the common good. This contingency, however, is of an
accidental nature, since in most normal circumstances,
the public good will not demand the public ownership
of industry. From the teachings in *Mater et Magistra*, it
is clear that under the natural law, property can be
owned either in a strictly private capacity or in a social
capacity (par. 117). In modern Western societies, the
socialized form of ownership manifests itself in limited
juridical operations called corporations in which ownership, properly speaking, is determined by shares in the
corporation itself. It is ruled by a special field of jurisprudence, called corporation law, which limits the corporation's liabilities. This socialized form of ownership
is fully compatible with social justice. Pope Pius XII
mentioned corporate organization in many of his dis-
courses, and gave his full approval to it, along with his
approval of ownership in the strictly private sense. Pope
John embraces this double approval in his own section
on private property and, for that reason, introduces
nothing new into the corpus of Catholic social thought.
With these two forms of ownership within the state, the
growth of intermediary bodies is encouraged and the
two extremes are avoided: namely, the dangerous concentration of most industry in the hands of a few, and
the equally dangerous monopoly by the state through
nationalization.

The socialization of ownership benefits the greatest
number of citizens in any society, largely because it has
the happy result of distributing the benefits of the
economy more equally to a greater number of citizens.

[19] See above, pp. 47–57.

Pope John and Pope Pius XII thus offer a middle course between capitalistic giganticism and state monopolization as a solution to the problem of ownership of the means of production or capital. Such progress in the concept of ownership of productive properties is a step forward from the tyranny of the few, and a step away from the tyranny of the many. This equalized and just view of the social order of John XXIII cannot be over-stressed.[20] Difficulties will always be present, but the general outline of a more equitable distribution and ownership of productive goods is available in this encyclical, though the practical application of the concept on a wide basis remains to be implemented. To encourage this implementation, the Pope calls this effort toward the socialization of property, shares, profit-sharing, and so on, a movement towards a truly human society of persons:

> Our predecessor, Pius XII, remarked that *the economic and social function which every man aspires to fulfill demands that the activity of each be not completely subjected to the will of others.* A humane view of the enterprise ought undoubtedly to safeguard the authority and necessary efficiency associated with unity of direction. It does not follow that those who are daily involved in an enterprise must be reduced to the level of mere silent performers who have no chance to bring their experience into play. They must not be kept entirely passive with regard to the making of decisions that regulate their activity. (Par. 92.)

It is not simply the material ownership of the goods of

[20] J. C. Cort, "The World of Work" in *The Challenge of Mater et Magistra* (New York, 1963), pp. 254–256.

production which is important in our highly organized society, but their effective management or use. The mere increase of a man's pay does not necessarily fulfill industry's obligations under the principles of social justice. Just as political systems have become more human by making the average citizen responsible for his political destiny, economic society must also be made more human by giving the worker more responsibility in what he produces. A voice in the management of industrial affairs is what makes an enterprise truly human, for only through a real control of the reins can responsibility be exercised by both the workers and the directors of the industry. Without this kind of responsibility, an economic society is clearly not humane, and to that extent, not in conformity with the natural law or the social teachings of the Church.

In its insistence on worker responsibility, the Pope's teaching aims at making society a more humane place in which to live, work, and attain salvation. Unfortunately, some have welcomed this part of the encyclical—and indeed the whole encyclical—as a victory "for" liberals over conservatives, or welfare-statesmen over decentralists. The perpetuation of this claim has been a disservice to the social teachings of the Church. Yet the particular value of this papal letter—and of all papal social teaching—is the insistence that, in striving for the common good, the dignity of the individual human person cannot be neglected. Rather than a victory for any partisan faction, the encyclical, especially in its insistence on human responsibility, is an "exciting new frontier of human endeavor that holds out unprecedented gains for mankind: gains that would abolish the roots of class warfare in society, of colonial wars, of nationalist wars; gains that would be as moving and fundamental as the history of the victory over slavery and famine."[21] From this vantage point, the Pope can see the future in optimistic terms, and, unlike the "prophets of doom," he does not deprecate our generation and civilization.

In any case, emphasis in our day has noticeably switched from the ownership of property to the effective control of property. In *Quadragesimo Anno,* Pius XI vigorously pointed to this shift. He noted that a few men in key positions could control the economy by setting prices, giving or withholding credit, under- or over-producing, and so on. This spirit is not entirely dead. In 1963, President Kennedy prevented the steel concerns from increasing prices at their own pleasure without considering the inflationary effect that steel would have on the rest of the nation's economy. Whether he was right or not does not dismiss the fact that the ownership or management of large industries involves a serious responsibility to the public welfare. This responsibility is doubly important because of the intimate socialization and interdependency of the economy. One of the ways to counteract irresponsible control in the hands of a few is to broaden the base of responsibility, thus of control.

> 113. It is not enough to assert the natural character of the right of private property, including productive property; strenuous efforts also must be made to see that the ability to exercise this right is extended to all social classes.

To emphasize this need, the Pope repeats the words of Pius XII that urge "the conservation and protection of social order which makes it possible for all citizens of every class to enjoy a secure, even if modest measure of ownership" (par. 114). In that same Christmas address,

[21] J. A. Raftis, *Social Order,* 12 (December, 1962), p. 456.

Pius XII concludes that this ownership will "promote higher education for the children of the working class who are especially endowed with intelligence and good will, will promote the care and the practice of the social spirit in one's immediate neighborhood, in the district, the province, the people and the nation, a spirit which, by smoothing over friction arising from privileges or class interests, removes from the workers the sense of isolation through the assuring experience of a genuinely human and fraternally Christian solidarity."[22] This is a clear insight into human psychology. No one takes great interest in the quality and caliber of anything unless it is —in part at least—his own. In large industries, the worker is in danger of isolation, of being a cog or number on the industrial scale, and this is disastrous not only for his dignity in work but for the rest of his attitudes in life. When effective responsibility is removed, so is the will to improvement, to industry, to self-dignity; and without these, the worker "sells" himself and his work to an industry for a wage and nothing more. To counteract this economic prostitution, the Pope insists that "today more than ever the wider distribution of private ownership ought to be forcefully championed" (par. 115).

The right of public authorities to regulate private groups so that they conform to the public good is clearly taught by John XXIII:

> 104. During these last decades, as is known, in the larger economic units there has come an increasingly pronounced separation of the ownership of productive goods from managerial responsibility. We know that this creates difficult problems of supervision for public authorities. For they have

---

[22] *The Major Addresses of Pius XII*, II (St. Paul, 1961), p. 62.

the duty to make certain that the aims pursued by the directors of leading companies, especially those having the greatest impact on the national economy, are not contrary to the demands of the common good. It brings about problems which, experience shows, arise regardless of whether the capital that makes possible these vast undertakings belongs to private citizens or to public agencies.

The activity of the public authority, which is more vast and complicated today than in times past, is justified by the principle of subsidiarity:

> 117. In modern times there is an evident tendency toward a progressive transfer of property to the state or other agencies of public law. The explanation of this tendency is to be found in the ever-widening activity which the common good requires that public authorities undertake. But even in this eventuality, the principle of subsidiarity stated above is to be faithfully observed. Accordingly, the state and other agencies of public law should not extend their ownership except where evident and real needs of the common good dictate it. And they should be on guard against extending it to the point where private property is excessively reduced or, even worse, abolished. (Also see par. 53, 104.)

Workers themselves, however, can participate actively in running and owning the industry to which they contribute their labor. Though just wages are a preliminary demand of social justice, the fullness of the workers' human dignity demands much more. According to Pius XI, the result of a common effort ought to be shared commonly.

91. Following the line of thought of Our predecessors, We defined the desire of employees to participate actively in the management of enterprises in which they are employed. It is not feasible to define a priori the manner and extent of participation of this sort. Such matters must be decided with an eye to specific conditions prevailing in each enterprise. These conditions vary from enterprise to enterprise, and, indeed, within the same enterprise frequently undergo sudden and profound changes.

We have no doubt, however, that workers should be allowed to play an active part in the affairs of an enterprise—private or public—in which they are employed. At any rate, every effort should be made that industrial enterprises assume the characterisics of a true human community whose spirit influences the dealings, duties and role of each of its members.

92. This indeed demands that relations between employers and directors on the one hand, and employees on the other, be marked by respect, appreciation, understanding, loyal and active cooperation, and devotion to their common undertaking. It also requires that the work be viewed and carried out by all the members of the enterprise, not merely as a source of income, but also as the fulfillment of a duty and the performance of a service to others. As a result, the workers should have a timely say in, and be able to make a welcome contribution to, the efficient development of the enterprise.

This participation in the industry, then, demands an effective voice in the running of that industry on all levels, managerial and directional as well as profit sharing.

97. Now, as is evident to all, in our day associations of workers have become widespread, and for the most part have been given legal status within individual countries and even across national boundaries. These bodies no longer recruit workers for purposes of strife, but rather for pursuing a common aim. And this is achieved especially by collective bargaining between associations of workers and those of management. But it should be emphasized how necessary, or at least very appropriate, it is to give workers an opportunity to exert influence outside the limits of the individual productive unity and indeed within all ranks of the commonwealth.

98. The reason is that individual productive units, whatever their size, efficiency, or importance within the commonwealth, are closely connected with the over-all economic and social situation in each country, whereon their own prosperity ultimately depends.

The vision of the Pope is startling. To the doctrinaire *laissez-faire* capitalist, this will appear as "socialism." In reality, it is a vision of perhaps the most effective form of democracy that the world has ever known. Political democracy alone does not correspond to the full dimensions of human nature; it must be supplemented with economic democracy, where the dignity of man is promoted by the ownership of and the responsibility for what he does and produces.

Both dimensions of democracy are discussed by Pope John: in *Pacem in terris* he considers political democracy, and in *Mater et Magistra* economic democracy. In these two encyclicals, he presents a real theology of terrestrial realities, of a world made by God for men, not for cogs or economic slaves. He presents a vision of democracy where the total economic life of man can insure both dignity and security for the future; where both economic and political rights are equally promoted and protected. By a broader ownership of industries and enterprises and by various intermediary groups which the Pope has outlined, the economic power for human promotion is effectively in the hands of the citizens, and not in the hands of the few.

> Considering the present state of science and technology, no employer could claim that he is meeting the requirements of justice if he fails to take such steps as are scientifically necessary and technically possible to provide for the health and safety of the workers. Then, too, it must be pointed out that as the workers themselves attain to a higher level of education and culture, they arrive at a better understanding of the business and are capable of a greater degree of independence and initiative in their work. This advance on the part of the worker calls for a further adjustment in the matter of human relations and a larger share on the part of the workers in the management of enterprise with the result that the legislator could now step in to define the obligations of justice more clearly.[23]

Though the Pope's thought has many shades of meaning, its general tenor is definitely towards this type of economic democracy. The essential aspect of this thought is that each person in society receive sufficient

[23] L. Janssens, "World Justice" in *World Justice*, 1 (September 1959), pp. 14–20.

private property to retain his fundamental freedom and right of initiative. By this means, a worker's human dignity can be safeguarded and, thus, he can never be reduced to a mere instrument of production.

V

The word *democracy* is composed of the two Greek words *"demos,"* the people, and *"kratein,"* to govern. Thus a democracy is a government *by* the people and *for* the people. To say that a government by the people is *for* the people means that the government is for *all* the members who come under its province. And it means that all these members should be able to enjoy all the elements which are present in society. What man has produced by his equality, originality, and liberty must be shared by all. Government for the people is an ideal toward which man must direct his efforts to achieve.

The first element that is necessary in any truly democratic society is moral and social liberty. In the notion of liberty, the idea of a liberation is present, and thus it is something dynamic. Man has an intellect, a disinterested faculty which necessarily requires truth. When a person tells a lie, for example, his intelligence tells him he is doing so. This ability helps man to take a disinterested point of view in regard to his other interested tendencies (*i.e.*, tendencies that interest him immediately). A man can thus step back from what his tendencies urge him to and act according to truth, according to the objective meaning of his being. He can free himself. This kind of action is what St. Thomas calls moral liberty,[24] and this is what is meant by liberty in the full sense of the word. In psychological liberty, on the other

[24] J. Leclercq, *La Philosophie Morale de Saint Thomas* (Louvain, 1954), p. 191.

hand, man has a liberty of choice: that is, he can commit an act or not. He can do this or he can do something else. Yet in the full meaning of liberty, a man can take an objective view of his interested tendencies. He is not condemned to follow his instincts. His intelligence is present to show him how to act and how to choose according to the objective meaning of his being.

Because the human person is irreplaceable, true liberty must be attained by the person himself; society cannot realize moral liberty for him, but can only create favorable conditions for the exercise of this freedom. In creating these conditions, society allows its members what is called social liberty. Here, the state must insure the conditions which are needed for all of the members to realize their moral liberty. These necessary conditions fall into two categories: political democracy and social democracy.

Within a system of political democracy, the essence of the rights of all the members is protected. The duly constituted public authority proclaims and vindicates the rights of all citizens. This system differs from a system of totalitarianism, where the personal rights of the people are not recognized. In such a system, the rights of the people are considered the property of the state. Thus such things as sterilization, euthanasia, unjust imprisonment, political executions and so on are permitted. Political democracy stands in direct opposition to totalitarianism. Based on universal elections, political democracy presupposes liberty of opinion, of communication, of association, freedom to belong to one association or political party rather than another, to choose whom one thinks the worthiest candidate, to hold meetings, and other concomitant freedoms. In such a system, then, a man's personal rights are respected by his representatives; if not, new representatives will be elected in their place (cf. *Pacem in terris,* par. 54–60).

Often, however, political democracy can provide only a negative social liberty. It is negative for those who do not have the means to enjoy the rights respected by the state. For example, the right to property is respected in a political democracy; but for the poor, this liberty is negative—that is, they do not have the means to exercise this right. The same applies to the right to work: this liberty is only negative for those who cannot find work. Because the effective exercise of liberty is often lacking in political democracy, something else must be added, and this something is social democracy.

While political democracy recognizes and protects the rights of individual citizens, social democracy insures that these rights can be exercised by all, and not just the privileged few. Under social democracy, social liberty becomes a positive reality; so in effect, political and social democracy cannot be separated. There can be little hope for peace and stability anywhere unless freedom has a substantial base. As outlined in *Pacem in terris*, political democracy demands not only periodic elections, but also a freedom from want and a freedom to education. Without adequate food, shelter, and health care, the existence of the right to vote can be the open door for the demagogue who promises Eden; and without an education, the responsibility for self-government is crippled at the start. Moreover, any country where the difference in wealth between the rich and poor is unjustly great, dissension, envy, and chaos have a fertile seed-bed.

In most countries in Latin America, for example, the granting of political democracy can hardly be effective. The inequalities in wealth, education, and power militate against order and stability. Though the Alliance for Progress attempts to help rectify these inequities, a steady and determined expense of time, effort, and patience is necessary on this continent where the privileged few and military dictatorships have ruled for over one hundred years. From a realistic point of view, political democracy in Latin America must be considered a long-range goal, and to achieve that goal, Americans must withstand many irritating and agonizing trials. Those who object, for example, that the Alliance for Progress should withdraw from countries that have not achieved or that even actively suppress political democracy, fail to recognize that if the people in these countries do not achieve a basic standard of living and education, the true basis for effective political democracy will never exist. Americans face a calculated risk, but one worth taking. For in such countries, the proclamation of human rights is empty verbiage when a truly human life is not possible. The right to work is meaningless if there are no jobs; the right to trade is nonsense if there are no goods to buy and no money to buy them with; and the right to private property is an insult to a man who is not allowed a plot of ground on which to scratch out an existence. The practical danger is very clear: All of these freedoms are necessary for man to achieve his proper dignity and worth, but if they cannot be exercised under what pretends to be political democracy, any social panacea that promises their exercise will win support.

To promote political democracy, then, social democracy must also exist: the former to recognize and protect human rights, and the latter to insure their proper exercise. As Pope John states in *Pacem in terris,* human rights are "universal, inviolable and inalienable" (par. 9); in essence, all men are absolutely equal in their claim to these human rights. But since each man is irreplaceable, his own capabilities and talents will determine how he exercises these rights. His own interior development cannot be demanded by the state, yet the state can prepare the proper external conditions to encourage this development—it can prepare the soil for a fruitful realization of positive liberty.[25]

The state has a mission to accomplish because it must concern itself with the social question. The phrase *social question* reminds us of the former problems between employers and employees, and this is understandable since it was the conditions and problems of the workers that gave birth to this term. *Rerum Novarum* was occasioned by the abuse of the industrial worker; *Quadragesimo Anno,* by the financial dictatorship emerging from capitalism. As a result, the tendency has been to teach these social encyclicals only in the context of crises. The workers fought for obtaining the external conditions needed for the progress of their subjective culture. In its true dimensions, however, the social question is much more extensive.

To speak of the social question and of a social democracy, two elements must be present. First, each man works according to his capacities.[26] All who are capable have the obligation to work since they must produce objective culture. Only through collaborating with each other can men realize the material well-being necessary for a truly human life. Second, each man must have at his disposal the means to develop his subjective culture. No exterior agent, human or otherwise, can develop a man's subjective culture for him; he must do it himself, but he must be able to find in society the conditions that make this possible. In other words, the objective culture

[25] See *Pacem in terris,* par. 18–22.
[26] *Ibid.,* par. 11, 18.

which is realized in society must be at the disposal of all. Each man must have what might be called fundamental goods; and without them, he cannot fulfill his personal destiny. These fundamental goods come from the exercise of three principal rights: the right to use economic goods, the right to the care of one's health, and the right to education. Since these are the elementary needs of every human life, every human being, no matter who he is, has a personal right to these "fundamental goods." The establishment of these conditions ought to inspire political action in every social democracy which is concerned with the more equitable distribution of the national revenue, the organization of medical care to assure the protection of the health of all, and the necessary means for procuring for all children the education suitable to their capabilities.

In order for these fundamental goods to be available, the objective culture must have reached a certain mimimal level. For each man to have the use of economic goods, a certain amount of these goods must be present. Until the nineteenth century, for instance, there were great famines in which thousands of people died miserable deaths. Because technical and scientific means were not adequately developed, economic conditions were so bad that misery was the law of a great part of society. Today, however, when technology and science have progressed rapidly and agriculture produces abundantly, it is now possible to apply the principle that all must enjoy the right to use economic goods. In a radio broadcast on the fiftieth anniversary of *Rerum Novarum* (Pentecost, 1941), Pius XII maintained that, since the national economy is the responsibility of each state and since it is the fruit of the collaboration of the state's members (objective culture), the end of the national economy is to assure the uninterrupted material conditions which are needed for all of the state's members to develop themselves fully. If this is realized in a durable way, the people of a country will be economically rich because all will have the right to use the goods of this world. If only the privileged have these goods, however, a country cannot be said to be economically rich. On the other hand, if material abundance is equitably distributed for the good of all, the people can be said to be economically rich and healthy.

The principles underlying a more equal distribution of property, ownership, and national revenues are clear in the social teaching of the Church. The practical implementation of these principles is left to individual countries. In America, the Anti-Poverty Program, the growing number of retaining agencies, the greater aid to institutions of higher learning (grants, scholarships, low-interest loans), the future prospect for some relief of high hospital costs for the aged through Medicare, the increasing degree of profit sharing—all these and other programs indicate ways in which the ideals are made realities. The Pope reminds us, however, that such a program will meet with stiff opposition:

> 229. The transition from theory to practice is of its very nature difficult. This is notably true when one tries to reduce to concrete terms the Church's social doctrine. And no wonder, in view of the deep-rooted selfishness of human beings, the materialism that pervades so much of modern society and the difficulty of determining the demands of justice in particular cases.

The examination of the right to private property in this Chapter has led to a discussion of the whole social fabric of modern society. This is not strange, for the reality of private property in all of its forms remains basic to any social reconstruction. Private property, in a sense, is the material "stuff" through which man expresses his incarnate personality and by which he achieves his human dignity. Small wonder, then, that the Pope spent so much of his time discussing this key element of social and economic reconstruction.

VI

Serious thinking on a Christian concept of work is relatively recent, even though secularists have long had it in their thoughts. Karl Marx was not the first man to theorize about work, but he was the first to study it systematically and thereby to produce a true philosophy of work within the Hegelian dialectic. His peculiar genius was to understand the central importance of work as a basic human value and drive. Marx's genius, however, was intimately connected to many erroneous social and metaphysical doctrines, and thus his philosophy of work was necessarily rejected by Christian thinkers. A negative attitude toward material things and novel opinions had been at work in Christian thought since the Council of Trent (1545–63), and, until *Rerum Novarum* and *Quadragesimo Anno,* no real attention was paid to the Christian meaning of work. But even the concern of Leo and Pius centered on the conditions and rights of the worker rather than on any theological significance of work as a human reality. Pope John gives this concept much broader development and attention.

Human work takes precedence by right and by dignity over the material means of production. This precedence exists because material things are a means to an end, whereas work is an end in itself since a man expresses his proper personality most intimately through it. That is why the Pope notes that progress has become more human in modern times because men have more confidence in their professional and technical skills today than they have had in former times.

106. Finally, it is noted that today men strive to acquire professional skills rather than to become owners of property. They have greater confidence in income derived from work or rights founded on work than in income derived from capital or rights founded on capital.

107. Moreover, this is in conformity with the superior nature of work since it is the immediate product of a human person. Capital, on the contrary, must be regarded as by its nature merely an instrument. Such a view of work may no doubt be considered a step forward in the process of human civilization.

In a remarkable passage, Pius XII said much the same thing: "Capital and its desire for gain determine what the needs of man should be and to what extent they are to be satisfied. Therefore, it is not human labor in the service of the common welfare that attracts capital to it and presses it into service; rather, capital tosses labor and man himself here and there like a ball in a game."[27] The Pope's indictment of the capitalistic system is very strong. It sounds very much like that of Karl Marx, who cried out that man's work is not a commodity to be sold on the market like other commodities. Man's work is of infinite worth. And the voice of a stranger and an atheist had to remind the Christian conscience of this basic perversion in nineteenth-century capitalism. Yet the tendency to undermine the true worth of work has not ceased. This type of assembly-line, automaton worker is

[27] *The Major Addresses of Pius XII*, I, p. 99

against the nature of man: he is not performing human work. In a basic sense, man exists for personalistic work; and capital exists for man—not the reverse, which was and is so prevalent in automated societies.

To a great degree, the thought of John XXIII emphasizes the concept and dignity of work rather than the more material aspects of the social order such as capital and private property. Because of the Incarnation, the position of human work in the social order is central. God became Man and thus all human activity has become a matter of grace. If work takes on a human consistence, it enters into the economy of grace; it enters as the work of man and under the principle of the community, which is also a means of grace. Through the continuous nature of the Incarnation in the Mystical Body of Christ, the world of work finds its equilibrium and its Christian place and is not simply regarded as an acquisition of merits.[28]

This incarnational aspect of work is central to the thought of John XXIII. The human community must make work its center because work is the most intimate expression of man's earth-bound personality. Human work produces the necessities and the security for man's existence, but in addition, man expresses his incarnational personality by work. The former two results of work were stressed by Leo XIII and Pius XI; the latter was stressed by Pius XII, and even more by John XXIII. It is this aspect of work, according to Pope John, which makes work such a profoundly human activity.

18. First and foremost, they concern work, which ought to be valued and treated not just as a commodity but as something which has on it the stamp of a human person. For the great majority of

[28] M. P. Chenu, *Pour une Théologie du travail* (Paris, 1955), p. 15.

mankind, work is the only source from which they draw their means of livelihood. Thus, the question of fixing a remuneration for labor cannot be left to the mechanical play of market forces. Instead, payment should be determined by standards of justice and equity. Otherwise, justice would suffer great harm even if the work contract should have been freely entered into by both parties.

Each human being must find a true expression of himself through his work or else it is nothing more than a brutal chore which offers neither dignity nor responsibility. Such a chore and the system that promotes it are unjust.

83. It follows that if the organization and operation of an economic system are such as to compromise the human dignity of those who engage in it, or to blunt their sense of responsibility, or to impede the exercise of personal initiative, such an economic system is unjust. And this is so even if, by hypothesis, the wealth produced through such a system reaches a high level and this wealth is distributed according to standards of justice and equity.

The Pope himself offers an exalted notion of work:

259. For this reason we strongly urge Our children everywhere, both clerical and lay, to remain thoroughly conscious of the extent of their dignity and high rank. These, in fact, are based on their oneness with Christ as branches with a vine: *I am the vine, you are the branches,* and on their ability to share in His divine life.

Hence, when Christians put themselves to work

—even if it be in a task of a temporal nature—in conscious union with the divine Redeemer, every effort becomes a continuation of the effort of Jesus Christ and is penetrated with redemptive power: *He who abides in me, and I in him, he bears much fruit.* It thus becomes a more exalted and more noble labor, one which contributes to a man's personal spiritual perfection, helps to reach out and impart to others on all sides the fruits of Christian redemption. It further follows that the Christian message leavens, as it were, with the ferment of the Gospel the civilization in which one lives and works.

Men are called upon to sanctify themselves by and through their work, not in spite of it. Too often in the past, sanctity has been separated from temporal activities to the detriment of both man and his Christian engagement.

Though the dehumanizing elements of some forms of work cannot be neglected, what is needed today more than a negative critique is this positive approach of John XXIII. Through the optimistic view presented in his letter, the spirituality of work takes on a new light. In co-operating with God in and through work, explains the Pope, man fulfills God's work, for the supernatural will build well on what has been naturally well formed. Fraternal charity is enhanced because the Christian, by his work, helps to contribute to the common cause of man here on earth, and is thus contributing to the cause of Christ in His mystery on earth. Above all, the challenge of modern life must be made spiritual through the organization of men in their work. In a beautiful passage, the Pope points out the spiritual fulfillment to be discovered by our work with others:

257. Whenever temporal affairs and institutions serve to further man's spiritual progress and advance him toward his supernatural goal, it can be taken for granted that they become at the same time more capable of achieving their immediate specific ends. Indeed, the words of our divine Master are still true: *But seek first the kingdom of God and His justice, and all these things shall be given you besides.* For the man who has become, as it were the *light of the world* and goes about *as a son of light,* has a surer instinct for grasping the fundamental demands of justice in different areas of human endeavor, even in those which are further complicated by the existence of widespread individual, group or racial selfishness. It should be added that one who is animated by Christian charity cannot help loving others and thus feeling the needs, suffering and joys of others as his own.

Consequently, aid from such a person, no matter what the circumstances in which it may be proffered, cannot but be more steadfast, more energetic, more humane and more disinterested. For charity is *patient, is kind; charity does not envy, is not pretentious, is not puffed up, is not ambitious, is not self-seeking, is not provoked; thinks no evil, does not rejoice over wickedness, but rejoices with the truth; bears with all things, believes all things, hopes all things, endures all things.*

Work must then be viewed both as a human task and as a continuation of God's initial command: "Dominate . . ." As his instrument, work liberates man both from his egoism and his brute surroundings. Viewed in this way, work is no longer a brutal juxtaposition of individuals, but a spiritual presence which, by a fraternal instinct, develops into a sort of social temperature never before felt. Work is that human activity which brings reason out of chaos and which transforms physical and brute reality into a human reality worthy of man.[29] The Pope's thought here is very close to that of Pierre de Chardin: the world is God's gift to man, but a gift that man must personalize and give back to God in perfected form. As the book of Genesis tells us, man is God's lieutenant, prolonging the act of creation here on earth. The Pope's whole view of the temporal order is in this vein.

Socialization, in the Pope's thinking, has made possible the great advances in communication, economy, and industrialization which are essential to man's occupation of this planet, to his wresting the earth from the forces of brute, non-intelligent nature; they allow him to convert the earth into a place where he may develop his talents and his total personality more easily and more completely. But, adds the Pope, for the Christian there is another aspect to work: it is a continuation of the work of Christ within the Mystical Body, a continuation of Christ Himself as he ministers to the basic needs of men all over the earth. The truly religious man cannot escape into a fake "supernaturalism" which is free from man's earthly agonies and pains. To the Pope, such a picture of Christianity is a caricature. Because of his deep sense of justice and charity, the Christian feels more intensely the manifold injustices in society, the pains and agonies of modern man.

In this context, the Christian's work becomes the saving instrument of Christ in the world to mitigate and abolish the sufferings of men and women. The Pope's view of the earthly city of man's work is not an escape,

---

[29] W. Ong, *Frontiers in American Catholicism* (New York, 1957), p. 88.

but a commitment to man and the modern world.[30] He calls on Christianity once again to become incarnate in the life and work of man. He rejects the over-long exploitation by capitalism that construes a man as a simple means of gain; he rejects the debasement of man by socialism (particularly communism), which has made man's work an irony, liberating him to become a slave to the state. In the vision of John XXIII, work frees man from the slavery of economic determinism, mechanistic monotony, and natural calamities (famines, droughts), but it is also redemptive because it is identified with Christ in the union of fraternal charity with his brothers here on earth for and through their needs.

[30] J. Villain, "L'Encyclique 'Mater et Magistra,'" *Revue de l'action Populaire,* 151 (1961), p. 912–913.

CHAPTER FOUR

Agriculture

I

SOME COMMENTATORS have claimed that the Pope's observations and comments on agriculture are the most important as well as the best informed in the whole letter. The agrarian problem is certainly very grave. Even in the United States, each successive administration has failed to provide a satisfactory solution to balance the agricultural economy with that of the rest of the country. In underdeveloped countries, the problem is somewhat different. Often, large tracts of land are owned by a few wealthy proprietors, and the majority of the farmers are nothing more than sharecroppers on these wealthy *latifundias*. While the Pope does not directly speak of agrarian reform, his concept of family farms as the ideal is certainly in this direction. This ideal has given fresh impetus to the agrarian reform movement throughout Latin America. As one writer put it, "There is not a bishop in all of Latin America today who does not stand four-square behind land reform."[1] The problem, however, is more complicated than this. In many places in Latin America, a simple and equal division of the land would result in farms so small that the techniques of modern farming (so necessary for

[1] D. Hyde, "First, the Land" in *Commonweal*, 75 (Dec. 22, 1961), p. 334.

modern economy) would be rendered impossible. This latter problem suggests the need for the kind of co-operatives among farmers that the Pope praises in this section of *Mater et Magistra*.

Under the principle of justice, each sector of the economy has the right to share equally with every other sector the higher standard of living due to increased production. Because of the industrial revolution, however, metropolitan areas have not only become the centers of population and industrialization, but also the principal beneficiaries of economic and social betterment. Rural areas both in the United States and in other countries have not kept pace with the growth in the rest of the economy; in fact, because of the agricultural revolution, they have actually fallen behind. Even the period from 1909 to 1914, in which agriculture enjoyed relative economic parity with the rest of the economy, the average annual income per person engaged in agriculture was less than that of other workers. In 1910, the average farm worker was earning two dollars to every three that the average factory worker earned. In 1960, the average annual farm income per person was down to two fifths of the average annual factory wage. This inequity is one of the main reasons why agriculture has become a depressed area. When agriculture cannot correct the problems which beset it, moreover, the public authority has a clear obligation to provide necessary assurances and stimulation. The principle is clear in *Mater et Magistra*:

73. Whereas in our era the economies of various countries are evolving very rapidly, more especially since the last great war, we take this opportunity to draw the attention of all to a strict demand of social justice, which explicitly requires that, with

the growth of the economy, there occur a corresponding social development. Thus, all classes of
citizens will benefit equitably from an increase in
national wealth. Toward this end vigilance should
be exercised and effective steps taken that class
differences arising from disparity of wealth not be
increased, but lessened so far as possible.

128. In addition, the economic systems of nations ought to be developed gradually and a balance maintained among all the sectors of production. That is to say, agriculture should receive
special help, in order to permit it to use the newly
devised methods of production, types of farm management and cultivation that the economic system
as a whole allows or requires. As far as possible, all
these innovations should be introduced in agriculture as much as in the industrial and service sectors.

The difficulty of applying this principle to agriculture
becomes obvious in the examination of one concrete
example, that of the Nigerian economy. Nigeria is strug-
gling to develop its economy and to create an equitable
distribution of wealth, but only among the industrial
and governmental classes. The agricultural classes are
almost totally neglected in the attempt to increase each
class share in the general productivity, but as the Pope
says, such neglect is contrary to the strict demand of
social justice.

Organized labor in Nigeria, the most populous African state south of the Sahara, is no longer prepared to
work for peanuts (even though peanuts are the Nigerian Federation's best-known crop). When a government commission suggested that workers should receive
minimum wages, doubling the pay of some, the govern-

ment declared that the enactment of this proposal would ruin the country. Instead, it offered a 20% increase in pay. Almost a million workers struck, and, after thirteen days at a standstill, the government agreed to negotiate on the basis of the commission's proposals. The meaning of these events is that the Nigerian revolution of expectations, which was roused during the agitation for an end to British colonialism, exploded in the face of the conspicuous consumption displayed by Nigerian politicians and their friends. After independence, Nigeria's new leaders set out to build a modern economy which was almost unrelated to Nigeria's traditional peanut economy. In the process they somehow managed to build themselves $180,000 "official" residences and luxury hotels for tourists, but the mud huts, the slums in the capital city, and the growing number of unemployed remained. Prices, rents, and politicians' pay have all gone up since independence, but not workers' wages. The politicians explain that it is impossible to increase investments and consumption at the same time. They preach austerity, but only the workers and the peasants practice it.

The answer to Nigerian poverty is to increase the average Nigerian's productivity, which everyone concedes to be appallingly low. But this cannot be done without providing the worker with both training and tools: this means capital investments. The country's "modern" economy has not directed money into improved farming or into small-scale manufacturing because the consumption patterns of the new elite have prevented the accumulation of capital. To redirect the money now being wasted into the hands of organized labor would simply be to share it with a would-be elite, for the farmers who comprise more than 80% of the population are not organized. The $1.9 billion allotted for industrial development under Nigeria's current four-year plan may come largely out of the farmers' hides. If the government grants wage increases to organized labor, it may stave off an industrial explosion, but it will further embitter farmers, the greater number. Social justice demands that austerity be applied to all the sectors of the economy and that any increased division of wealth also be shared by all: workers, farmers, and services (including public service). Without such a program, not only will certain parts of the economy become depressed, but social unrest will also develop.

In the economically underdeveloped countries, unevenly developed economies and social unrest are particularly dangerous to the stability of the government. "It is this problem of maintaining balance among all sectors of the economy which impresses and disturbs John XXIII."[2] The Pope, however, cannot give minute and detailed plans to avoid this problem because economic and social conditions differ from one country to another. From a moral point of view, however, he gives the general principles that can lead to the expansion of the persons who draw their livelihood from agriculture. The Pope insists that agriculture, like industry, is to become "a community of persons" which leads to the personal expansion of its members through freedom and responsibility.

The problems of agriculture in the United States are serious. Between 1940 and 1960 migration from the farms averaged almost one million persons a year. Today the total United States rural population is slightly less than 16% of the total population. These figures represent a drop of almost 50% in twenty years, and at present, there is no sign that the movement is

[2] L. N. Hamel, " 'Mater et Magistra': One Conception" in *Culture*, 22 (December, 1961), p. 425.

going to stop. All this migration is not an absolute evil, since much of it has been due to the agricultural revolution of the past fifty years. New machines, fertilizers, insecticides, and scientific farming techniques have allowed fewer farmers to produce more. Each year, in fact, a new bumper crop is stored in United States government bins and granaries. This agricultural abundance has been advantageous to the consumer, and today he spends less than one-fifth of his income for food. The application of these modern farming techniques has increased food supplies, but it has also released millions of farm hands for work in the industrial sectors of the economy. Without this supply of labor, industry could never have progressed as it has in the past twenty years.

The agricultural sector of the community is of vital importance to the United States economy.[3] After all, food is the primary stuff of life, a basic necessity. This necessity is produced by 15 million persons for a population of well over 193 million. Besides its direct production of food, agriculture is important to the United States economy in other ways. The agricultural sector is one of the biggest customers of American business. Farmers spend over 40 billions dollars each year for machinery, petroleum, rubber products and services of all kinds. Moreover, the food processing industry employs over 10 million people, and as a result, four out of every ten workers are directly involved in food preparation and processing. Farmers not only produce more and better food; they create millions of jobs for American workers.

Yet agriculture is vulnerable. In its very nature, it

[3] We are grateful to the article by J. L. Vizzard, "The Farm Problems: Analysis and Answers" in *Social Order*, 12 (May, 1962), pp. 209–219, which is summarized in this section with permission.

depends on unstable and unpredictable factors such as the weather and supply and demand. Yet the agricultural revolution has allowed the farmer to outstrip demand. Thus the government buys much of the farm surplus and spends over a million dollars a day to store surplus food. If it were not for such government action, the farmer's income would be further reduced and would probably lead to a depression in agriculture comparable to that of the 1930's. Ironically, the means which have fostered greater productivity among farmers have also upset their market. Even with government action, there has been a drop in farm prices over the years. Between 1952 and 1960, farm prices dropped over one-fifth while the farmer's cost of production (improved seed, fertilizers, machinery, and so on) rose by more than one-sixth. Because of the high cost of upkeep and renovation, agriculture has fallen far behind the rest of the economy.

In an analysis of American agriculture, a distinction must be made between the large corporate farms (roughly half) and the small family farms, which are characterized by underdevelopment and low income.

> 142. In view of the diversity of rural conditions within each nation, and the even greater differences from nation to nation, it is impossible to determine a priori what the structure of farm enterprises ought to be. But if we hold to a sound natural, and even more so a Christian, concept of man and the family, we are forced to adopt as our ideal of a farm unit especially a family-type farm, one that resembles a community of persons, whose inner relations and structure conform to the standards of justice and Christian teaching.

The poorer farmers in America are falling further and

further behind the economic eight-ball. This condition leads to Pope John's observation that millions of farmers each year are abandoning rural life. Because of the lack of opportunity, four million American farm boys coming to maturity in the next fifteen years will attempt to find employment in industrial centers. According to the 1960 census, more than 1,500 rural counties actually lost population while the rest of the nation, particularly metropolitan areas, increased.

Pope John calls agriculture a depressed area; and it is, even in the United States. The average income of American farmers is well behind that of their fellow citizens located in industrial areas. Thirty-six percent of all families living on farms have gross annual incomes of less than $2,000. Furthermore, one third of all American farms are without telephones, while two-fifths of them are without running water. The construction of libraries, hospitals, and good roads has been increasing over the past few years, especially over the past thirty. Still, the situation is not at a parity.

While the economic return to the farmer for his goods has actually decreased, however, his output has vastly increased both in quality and quantity. Farm production in 1960 was almost 30% above that of 1946–1947. Yet the farmer's earnings only rose 13% during that time, not even enough to compensate for the decreasing value of the dollar. Consumer prices for food have been abnormally low—an increase of only two percent over the past ten years—and they have not kept pace with the 15% rise in wages and other costs. For example, wheat, small grains, and livestock producers have raised production by some 16%, but their incomes have actually decreased by some 28%. To grant the farmer a more equitable share in the gross national income, the consumer can well afford to pay a little more for his food.

American farmers fall into two large categories: one, about 50% of the farm population, the large corporative farmer who has organized and mechanized his farm and who produces about 90% of agricultural products; the second, about 45% of the farm population, the poor, uneducated, and unskilled farmer who grows less than 10% of agricultural produce. This so-called "agricultural proletariat" has been largely by-passed by the technological revolution in farming. Through the war on poverty, it can be retrained either for farming or for other sectors of the economy, or given easy credit and loans for modern equipment, or perhaps given outright grants for rebuilding its small, family-type farms.

The second group of farm workers who can be helped through the war on poverty are the migratory workers who, along with the Negroes and the Puerto-Ricans, are among the poorest and least trained of American workers. Making a bad situation worse, whole sectors of the business community actually import even poorer "wet backs" from Mexico to keep labor costs low. All attempts by Congress to check this flow of white slavery have been firmly checked. Until 1965 this national disgrace perpetrated by the so-called "conservatives" in Congress merits for each of them the "badge of infamy," in the words of Archbishop Lucey of San Antonio. The migratory workers desperately need minimal wage laws, social security and unemployment benefits, increased medical insurance, and some efficacious method of education for their children.

Reporting to Congress in 1964, the McCullen Committee made several practical recommendations which would alleviate the plight of the migratory worker. It recommended amendment of the Fair Labor Standards Act to remove agricultural exclusion; amendment of the Labor-Management Relations Act to guarantee farm workers the right to organize and bargain collectively; amendment of the Social Security Act to provide full coverage for agricultural workers; amendment of present immigration laws, or enactment of new ones, to block any future imported-labor program like the *bracero* system. It also recommended Federal action to aid the broadening of unemployment insurance laws and of welfare. These and other recommendations were nipped in the bud by the "conservative" members of Congress, arguing that to stop "wet backs" would be to cause a farm labor shortage. And yet millions of American farm workers leave the farms for the city because they cannot find adequately compensated work. Do the "conservatives" really mean a labor shortage or do they mean a shortage of men who will labor for almost nothing?

II

Though the American farmer has been able to produce more and better food, the reward for his production has not been forthcoming. Of every dollar spent for food, the farmer receives only 37 cents, while the rest is syphoned off by processors and distributors. The principal reason for this low return for the farmer's production comes from a persistent weakness in the farmer's market. Basically, the farmer lacks the power to bargain and is at the mercy of the packers and millers. Pope John offers a solution to this problem:

146. One should remember that in agriculture as in every other sector of production, association is a vital need. This is especially so where family-type

farms are involved. Rural workers should feel a sense of solidarity one with another, and should unite to form co-operatives and professional associations. Both types of organization are quite necessary if farmers are to benefit from scientific and technical progress in methods of production. The same is true if they are to contribute effectively toward maintaining prices for their products or if they are to attain an equal footing with other economic and professional classes, which are likewise usually organized. Then, too, if farmers organize they can exercise an influence on the conduct of public affairs proportionate to their status. For today almost nobody hears, much less pays attention to, isolated voices.

Like the factory worker, the farmer must organize and then utilize the power born of collective bargaining.

Professor K. Galbraith has called for rigorous government control of farm production to give the farmer more bargaining power.[4] This suggestion is perhaps too strong, but the idea has been finding more acceptance among American farmers. Working in the Corn Belt, the National Farms Organization is presently enlarging its membership to better its bargaining position with the packers. When such an organization has signed enough members, it can approach the millers and packers with effective demands for a bigger share of the food dollar. The NFO has already withheld some farm produce from the market, and the action has forced some packers to agree to collective bargaining. The farmers who agreed to withhold their hogs from the market conse-

[4] *American Capitalism: The Concept of Countervailing Power* (Boston, 1960), Ch. 11.

quently got what they wanted. Like industrial strikes, these withholding actions were effective; and also like strikes, they are in perfect agreement with the principles of social justice. More such organizations are needed in different sectors of the agricultural economy. Also needed is education in such organizations so that they can spread and be effective.

All statistics prove that the farmer's share in the profit made on food production is very low. Between 1952 and 1960, the retail price of milk went up about 2 cents a quart, but the farmer's return actually dropped 1 cent a quart. Consumers paid about 1 cent a pound more for American-made cheese, but the farmer received 6 cents less a pound. The retail price of butter fell 10 cents a pound, but it was the farmers who absorbed about 9½ cents of this drop. The farmer is not getting his fair share in the increased abundance of the American economy; and he is not only getting less, but he is actually subsidizing the American consumer. The question naturally poses itself: Why cannot the farmer regulate prices and production as business does? The answer lies in the very nature of agriculture.

Basically the economics of agriculture differ from those of industry and the services. To the superficial observer, economic law is the same whether it applies to the production of wheat, automobiles, or resort motels. When supply is short, prices tend to rise. When supply is excessive, prices drop until that over-supply is brought up. In practice, things are not that simple. The application of this basic law of supply and demand to three examples—automobiles, motels, and wheat—will show some revealing distinctions.

In the case of automobiles, manufacturers calculate the number to be supplied in advance on the basis of market surveys. The maker of compacts will try to estimate the future market for compacts, and then he will key production to that particular figure. He aims to produce precisely the amount that dealers can sell in the model year. If he sells this amount at a competitive price, he expects to make a profit. Should he fail to make a consistent profit, he either drops the model, changes it drastically, or perhaps goes out of business altogether. Only in the rare cases where the industry as a whole badly miscalculates the market is there a heavy surplus of automobiles at the end of the model year.

The resort motel builder is in somewhat the same position. He calculates the number of vacationers that can be attracted to an area. He notes the capacity of competitors whose motels would compare with his in quality and location. He tries to allow for the possibility that others might also build new motels in the area. If he thinks he has a reasonable chance of success, he goes ahead. He may prosper. Should he fail, he sells at a loss and the new buyer tries his luck. When a major mistake is made, the motel is abandoned.

In both these examples the owners were able to calculate the expected market and plan accordingly. They were not guaranteed success or immunity from competition, but most of the important factors were known and many were subject to their control. Even if the owners were disappointed in their first results, they often had a second chance. They could use advertising or price cuts to sell their product, hoping to recover their losses at a later time.

The economic problems of the wheat farmer are not so predictable. In the absence of government controls or widespread co-operative marketing, the farmer's method of operation will be quite different from that of the other businessmen considered. First of all, he can have little or no success in trying to calculate the market for his product or the price he expects to receive. There is nothing that he can do to adjust production to market demand and thus receive a reasonable price. The supply of wheat depends on two incalculable factors: the weather and the production from thousands of other farmers acting independently of him.

III

In the area of agriculture, then, government action is a practical necessity. The individual farmer, acting by himself, cannot have an appreciable effect on production or prices.

> 137. In view of the special nature of agricultural products, farm prices should be protected with the help of some of the many devices which economic experts have discovered. It is very desirable that such regulation be primarily the work of the interested parties; supervision by public authority, however, cannot be dispensed with.
>
> 138. On this subject it must not be forgotten that the price of agricultural commodities usually represents compensation for the farmer's work rather than a return on capital.

Coming from a family of farmers himself, Pope John had direct knowledge of what he is here talking about. Certainly government action in the area of agriculture ought to safeguard its basic unity. This was one of the salient characteristics of the "Brannan Plan" and, as such, was praiseworthy. For those who are supposedly so interested in preserving the free enterprise system, here is a perfect case in point: government action is needed to sustain individual initiative and individual continuation in agriculture.

If it is to bring about effective price controls, government action must insure effective production control. Without production control, the farmer always faces the danger of a glutted market and, thus, a low return for his produce. To insure against over-production, however, an effective control of the market is more important than any control of acreage. The control of acreage is always subject to the accidents in nature, while the demands of the market can be more accurately regulated and predicted. In 1955, Congress instituted the Rural Development Program (RDP) to aid the farmer in planning his production to meet the demands of the market and to find other ways to unload surplus production. Congress has also instituted other programs for effective use of surplus to stimulate the economy, such as the Food Stamp Program (and its extension and increase in 1964). Moreover, voluntary programs such as CARE and Food for Peace have been beneficial in helping people help themselves.

Despite continued reductions in the number of acres and man-hours devoted to food production, the American cornucopia continues to pour forth an increasing amount of food. The present farm output provides 12,000 calories per day for each man, woman, and child in the United States, or, to use the standard American diet, enough food to feed one billion people. American farmers feed some of this surplus to animals, thereby exchanging carbohydrate for protein calories. The United States also gives a great deal of food away and wastes a great deal of it; and still there are surpluses to keep in storage—from 50 to 60% of the annual production of all major grains. During the past fifteen years, these developments in production have confounded all efforts to manage American agriculture on economic principles predicated upon the assumption or the maintenance of scarcity. The United States agriculturist continues to talk orthodox classical (or scarcity) economics on Sunday, but he has meanwhile learned to practice a pragmatic kind of abundance economics on weekdays. Although he has not yet come to advocate anything so radical as production for use, he strongly favors production for production's sake.

In the past decade, one of the principal measures for sustaining the American agricultural economy against the crushing burden of its surpluses has consisted in shipping those surpluses overseas to feed the hungry. Since 1954, more than $9,000,000,000 worth, or seventy-five million tons, of agricultural commodities have been delivered to forty-four developing countries. Shipments of wheat alone have amounted to two entire bumper crops. Under the legal trickery of Public Law 480, which sanctions this use of surpluses, the food is sold to foreign governments at world prices. The payment is taken, however, in nonconvertible currency and is loaned back to the recipient government to finance economic development programs. Sunday economics is thereby satisfied by the assurance that two dollars are made to grow in the place of one, and Public Law 480 stands as one of the most secure statutes on the books.

By the food shipments sanctioned by Public Law 480, the benefits which have accrued to countries with developing economics are plain enough. The benefits to the American economy, however, can hardly be estimated. Under this law, Americans have shipped out commodities of unquestionable intrinsic value; yet it is impossible to find that it costs Americans anything. The farmer was paid for his produce. In fact, as a result of these shipments and their salutary effect on domestic commodity prices, our farmers received more than a billion dollars in extra income. Unburdening its storage bins in 1958 and 1959, the Federal government made "savings in price support acquisitions, storage and interest" totaling $545 million on shipments that costs $668 million. Because the law reserves such shipping to American bottoms, the U. S. Merchant Marine picked up nearly $250 million in extra revenues from Public Law 480 during the first three years of its administration. Looking to the future, the farmers and their packers and shippers cheer themselves further with the prospect that these shipments have opened up new export markets for later dollar sales of United States farm commodities.[5]

IV

In the Pope's discussion of agriculture, he bases his observations and recommendations on human values and their protection and promotion. Earlier in the encyclical, he said that, like industry, the agricultural sector must be viewed as a human community of persons and not as mere cogs in a vast machine.

> 85. Artisan enterprises and family-type farms, as well as the co-operatives that serve to supplement and improve them, ought to be preserved and fostered in accord with the common good and within the limits of technical possibilities.
> 89. Moreover, the measures taken by public agencies on behalf of craftsmen and members of co-operatives are also justified by the fact that these two categories of citizens uphold true human values and contribute to the advance of civilization.

Keeping his eye explicitly on the human values that

[5] In this respect, note the heated discussions in Congress (1965) over wheat shipments to Russia.

grow out of agriculture, the Pope states that family farms, farmers' associations, and professional organizations are all means to promote such values.

Working within the context of the possible, however, the Pope knows that migration of farm hands to the metropolitan areas is caused by the modernization of farming. To this extent, it cannot be stopped and any "back to the land" ideology is doomed in the modern world. But he also knows that part of the reason for this radical migration is that farming has become a depressed occupation. Farming income is not equal to that of the rest of society, and in many ways rural sectors are more backward than urban and metropolitan areas. In his discussion, the Pope first gives the realistic picture and then some remedies:

124. We all know that as an economy develops and flourishes, the labor force engaged in agriculture decreases. At the same time, the percentage of the labor force employed in industry and the services rises. Nevertheless, We think that the shift from farming to other productive sectors is often due to a variety of factors over and above those directly linked to economic development.

Chief among these factors may be listed a desire to escape from an environment considered as confining and devoid of prospects; the longing for novelty and adventure that has taken such a hold on the present generation; greed for quickly amassed riches; a yearning and thirst for a freer way of life and enjoyment of the comforts that more heavily settled areas and urban centers commonly afford. But it is undoubtedly true also that one of the motives behind this shift is the fact that the farm area, almost everywhere, is a depressed

one—whether one looks at the index of productivity of the labor force or the standard of living of
farm populations.

127. It is above all indispensable that great care
be taken, especially by public authorities, to insure
that the essential public services are adequately
developed in rural areas: good roads, transportation, means of communication, drinking water,
housing, health facilities, elementary education,
technical and professional training, provision for
the practice of religion and for recreation, and
finally, a good supply of those products needed to
insure that farm homes are furnished and equipped
to be run on modern lines.

Whenever such services, which are essential for a
decent standard of living on the farm, are lacking
to rural dwellers, socio-economic progress becomes
almost impossible or takes place too slowly. The
consequence is that the drift of population away
from the farms becomes almost impossible to check
and difficult to control.

If the farmer is thus a "second-class citizen," reasons
the Pope, he cannot consider his great vocation as a
good in itself. Two ways of promoting the farmer to
first-class citizenship are to decrease the difference of
income between rural and urban centers, and to make
available to the farmer such conveniences and facilities
as roads, hospitals, easy transportation, and recreational
centers. The Pope considers these services essential for a
decent standard of living: in their absence, the drift
from rural to urban centers will continue and the inferi-
ority complex of the farmer will increase. As stated
above, government action in America has helped improve the farmer's life, especially in the past thirty

years. In the United States, all of the Pope's recommendations have long since been followed by the creation of various agencies and administrations.

The Pope's recommendations, moreover, are practical for the total economy. American agriculture spends almost 40 billion dollars a year for goods and services from other areas of the economy, thus helping to stimulate other sectors of the economy. Yet the lowered farm income has had far reaching effects. For example, tractor production in 1960 was less than one-third that of 1951. Because of reduced sales, many of the 55,000 workers in the tractor industry no longer have jobs. The reduction in farm income had a direct effect on industrial income. Pope John clearly understands this interrelationship:

> 129. In this way, the agricultural economy comes to absorb a larger amount of industrial goods and to demand a higher quality of service. In turn, it offers to the other two sectors and to the whole community products which best meet, in quality and quantity, the needs of the consumer. In this way, it contributes to the stability of the purchasing power of money—a very helpful factor in the orderly development of the entire economic system.

Because of this interrelationship, the Pope observes that the whole economy must balance if it is to retain its health and vigor. And because agriculture is depressed, he suggests that corrective action be taken.

His specific recommendations are evident and direct. Justice demands the proportional or graduated tax laws, since the individual must contribute to the support of government only according to his means. In the case of farming—given the special risks and dangers—tax credits must be at least as generous as the 1964 tax cut has been on the renovation of machinery by corporations.

132. The fundamental principle in a system of taxation based on justice and equity is that the burdens imposed should be proportionate to the capacity of people to contribute.

133. In the assessment of taxes in rural areas, the common good requires that the government bear in mind that agricultural income flows in more slowly and is exposed to greater risks in the process of production, and that consequently there is greater difficulty in obtaining the capital necessary to increase income.

The Pope also suggests that social security can help balance the economy. But in the United States, farmers are not included in social security programs. Such programs are much more extensive in Europe, and, of late, there has been some talk in Congress of including farmers under social security. Distribution of wealth through social security programs is clearly approved by the Pope.

136. Systems of social insurance and social security can contribute effectively to the redistribution of national income according to standards of justice and equity. These systems can therefore be looked on as instruments of restoring balance between standards of living among different categories of the population.

The effect of social security is beneficial to the whole economy because it lowers the extremes of wealth and poverty in any one country. The wisest program for the stimulation of the farm economy is no doubt a combination of Pope John's recommendations: tax cuts to provide ready recovery for expenses and investment, and social security programs for protection and security. The thirty years of experience since the New Deal seem to indicate that these kinds of programs do benefit America. Yet it is the farmers themselves, aided by public authorities, who are to carry this program of economic revival to its completion.

144. It is Our opinion that farmers themselves as the interested parties ought to take the initiative and play an active role in promoting their own economic advancement, social progress and cultural betterment. These workers can readily perceive and appreciate the fundamental nobility of their work. It is carried on in the majestic cathedral of nature. It constantly deals with plants and animals, whose life is inexhaustible in its modes of expression, inflexible in its laws, rich in allusions to God, the Creator and Provider. And finally, it produces not only the variety of food needed to nourish the human family but also an increasing supply of raw materials for manufacturing.

The farmers must be organized and modern in their techniques, yet they must be helped to attain this end. On large farms where many men work under a managerial administration, a true community of persons does not usually exist. Though such large farms are necessary in certain cases, they certainly are not the ideal.

142. In view of the diversity of rural conditions within each nation, and the even greater differences from nation to nation, it is impossible to determine a priori what the structure of farm enterprises ought to be. But if we hold to a sound natural, and even more so a Christian, concept of

man and the family, we are forced to adopt as our ideal of a farm unit especially a family-type farm, one that resembles a community of persons, whose inner relations and structure conform to the standards of justice and Christian teaching. With this in mind, we should exert every effort to realize this ideal, as far as circumstances permit.

Like industry, farming is at its best when the workers themselves share in the effective ownership and management as well as the work. In this sense, the family-type farm gives the best hope of promoting human dignity. When the farmer rents rather than owns his farm, that too represents a certain loss of human value in farming. Public authorities ought to promote private ownership of farms through low-rate-interest loans and credits. Ownership will increase the farmer's personal pride and incentive; and to compete successfully with other farmers, he will be encouraged to have the most up-to-date machinery, techniques, and so on. In this too, public authorities will often have to help.

143. If a family-type farm is to survive, it must produce sufficient income to enable the family to live in decent comfort. To do this, it is very necessary that farmers be given special instructions, be kept constantly up-to-date and be supplied with technical assistance in their profession. It is also essential that they form a flourishing system of co-operatives and professional organizations. They ought likewise to take an effective interest in public affairs that concern not only administrative agencies, but also political movements.

Yet the best way for the farmer to improve his lot is through organization, because he retains the initiative for his own betterment. And only in this way can the farmer have a real bargaining power with millers and packers. Co-operatives offer him the protection he needs (par. 146).

Bringing his discussion of agriculture to a close, Pope John eulogizes the vocation of the farmer. In its very nature, farm life teaches a man the virtues of patience and responsibility.

> 145. Furthermore, farming has its own professional dignity, since indeed it involves the use of many things borrowed from technology, chemistry and biology, and these must constantly be adjusted to meet the demands of change, because scientific progress clearly has an important effect on farming.
>
> It is also a work characterized by its own moral dimension. For it demands of the farmer a capacity for orientation and adaptation, patience in the face of an uncertain future, a sense of responsibility toward the demands of the task at hand, a spirit of perseverance and initiative.

Urban life has its dangers and uncertainties, but no other sector, including business and industry, would cling to such a work if it had the economic drawbacks of farming. Farming is thus more than an occupation taken up to make a living. It is a vocation through which a man develops his personality and to which he gives all his talents and love. In the final analysis, it is only the love of farming that makes the farmer remain on his farm in spite of low income, an uncertain future, and risks of all kinds.

> 149. In farm work the human personality finds many aids to self-expression, self-development and

cultural enrichment. Therefore, the farmer should consider his work as a vocation and a mission. Moreover, he ought, as it were, to consecrate his labor to God, whose Providence directs all events to man's salvation. He ought finally to accept the assignment to elevate himself and others to a higher level of culture.

CHAPTER FIVE

Economically Underdeveloped Nations

I

POPE JOHN XXIII's INTERNATIONALISM is everywhere evident in both of his two monumental encyclicals, *Mater et Magistra* and *Pacem in terris*. In the latter, political evolution is uppermost; in the former, the question of international social justice and responsibility is of primary concern. Yet the two cannot be separated without destroying the integrity of Pope John's internationalism.

The teaching of the popes on internationalism and the desirability of world government under law is clear and forthright.[1] The obligation to form a world government does not come from the individual consent of nations (which is certainly necessary), but from the moral law itself. The individual states of the world are in a relationship to the world community as parts are to a whole: the parts are always subordinate to the common good of all men throughout the globe. Yet this relationship has not found acceptance. Catholic isolationalists, for example, who claim that what is good for the nation is good for the world, or that the United States must seek its own good without seriously considering the conse-

[1] E. Guerry, *The Popes and World Government* (Baltimore, 1963).

quences of such action on other countries, overlook this definite moral demand. Furthermore, the modern errors of materialism and pragmatism on both sides of the Iron Curtain have resulted in a proliferation of polluted illusions which, like skepticism and cynicism, are inadequate for guiding the builders of the international city of man. To state the problem directly, the present historic crisis lacks an ethical principle that can guide international society through the tangle of ideologies which threaten the destruction of man.

Since the whole of the human race is a true family under the Fatherhood of God (and this has never been used by the Church or the Popes as a mere metaphor), individual men and individual nations have a serious moral obligation to come to the economic aid of those who are less fortunate or less developed. The world's goods and resources have been created for all men, and not for any particular nation; thus the patrimony of the whole human race is the sum total of all the wealth of the individual nations. Within this understanding of the world's goods, the obligation of economically developed countries to help the underdeveloped countries is a matter of strict justice, and not of simple charity.

157. One of the most difficult problems facing the modern world concerns relations between nations that are economically advanced and those in the earlier stages of development. The former enjoy a high standard of living, while the latter countries suffer from extreme poverty.

The solidarity which binds all men and makes them members, in a sense, of the same family requires that nations enjoying an abundance of material goods should not remain indifferent to those nations whose citizens suffer from internal problems that result in poverty, hunger and an inability to enjoy even the more elementary human rights. This obligation is all the more urgent since, given the growing interdependence among nations, it is impossible to preserve a lasting and beneficial peace while glaring socio-economic inequalities persist among them.

158. Mindful of Our role of Universal Father, We feel obliged to repeat solemnly what We have stated elsewhere: *We are all equally responsible for the undernourished peoples. . . .* [Therefore] *it is necessary to awaken men's consciences to a sense of the responsibility which weighs upon everyone, especially upon those who are more richly blessed with this world's goods.*

This statement leaves no doubt that the wealthy countries are enjoined in conscience to help the poorer.

The wretched conditions that exist in the underdeveloped countries cannot be over-emphasized. The statistics are familiar, and yet these impersonal lists and charts often obscure the fact that each member or each symbol represents a living, suffering, individual human being. One must visit, or at least make a strenuous empathetic leap to, the crowded streets of Bombay or the *favelas* of Rio de Janeiro to experience the deep feelings which the Pope evinces in his plea for justice. Two thirds of the world's people are ill-fed, ill-clothed, and ill-housed. According to the most recent figures of FAO, thirty-five million people die each year from malnutrition. For these people, the major problem is not freedom or bondage, or even war or peace, but simply getting enough to eat each day to stay alive. Millions of children die each year from lack of food. In Pakistan alone over 60% of the children die before they reach the age of three years. In order to lead a normal life, food experts agree that the daily calorie intake must be at least 2,700. The average American and Northern European has more than 3,200 each day while the rest of the world has less than 2,200.

The lack of sufficient calories, however, is not the only problem. Many of the world's people lack not only quantity but also quality in the food they eat. In many countries this is due to the one-crop system superimposed on them by Western imperialism and colonialism of the not so distant past. In others, it is due to poor farming techniques, lack of hybrid and otherwise improved seed, and lack of irrigation for crop variety.[2] Several international organizations, both of the UN and of individual Church and philanthropic groups, have been attempting to remedy this situation, and the Pope encourages them in their gigantic task:

> 155. It is obvious that the solidarity of the human race and a sense of Christian brotherhood demand that an active and varied program of co-operative aid be established among the peoples of the world. They demand a co-operation which permits and encourages the movement of goods, capital and men with a view to reducing the above-mentioned imbalance. Later on, We shall treat this point in more detail.
>
> 156. At this point, however, We must express Our warm approval of the work which the United Nations Food and Agricultural Organization (FAO) has been doing. This organization has as its special objective to promote fruitful accord among

[2] N. Drogat, *The Challenge of Hunger* (Westminster, Md., 1962), pp. 14–53.

nations; to encourage the modernization of agriculture in underdeveloped nations; and to alleviate the suffering of hunger-stricken peoples.

FAO has helped poor countries to achieve variety in diet, better balance between agriculture and trade, longer life span, reduced infant mortality rates, and better health in general. UN technicians have helped to improve the quantity and quality of food by showing farmers new methods of farming, such as crop rotation, the use of fertilizers, and the use of hybrid seed. Yet much remains to be done. Here is the witness of one author:

> At Lima, almost a third of the population lives in cities of planks and sheet iron that the people there call *las barruadas*. There is one water tap for every hundred families. But in the center of the city the golf course is so carefully watered that one might believe it had been imported from rainy England. In Rio de Janeiro, the name *favellas* is given to the slums of about 80,000 inhabitants each which surround the city. A third of the population lives in them.
>
> At Caracas, 400,000 people live in the *barrios;* and when I expressed my amazement at them and pictured a revolt of these thousands of wretched people, those to whom I was talking replied calmly: "They are but half men; a machine gun would set them fleeing."[3]

If the American people were shocked at the condition of the migrant workers depicted in *Grapes of Wrath,* what would they do if they saw and experienced an

---

[3] R. Scheyven, *De Punta del Este à la Havane* (Paris, 1960), p. 112.

infinitely worse situation in South American *favellas?*[4]
This is only one section of the world. Yet the story is all
too familiar: Egypt, Viet Nam, Brazil, Jordan, China.

The moral obligation to help the world's poor is clear.
Pope John is adamant in impressing this obligation on
the rich:

> 161. Everyone is aware that some countries have
> a surplus of consumer goods—especially farm pro-
> duce—while in other lands large segments of the
> population suffer from hunger and want. Justice
> and humanity demand, then, that the rich come to
> the aid of the poor. To destroy or to squander goods
> that other people need for survival goes against all
> canons of equity and human kindness.

Each year the American government spends a billion
dollars to pay farmers for not growing food and to buy
up and store the surpluses they do grow. As explained in
the previous chapter, the exportation of such surpluses
injects new life into the American agricultural economy
and saves the taxpayers millions of dollars each year.
From a practical point of view, Food for Peace has bene-
fited the American taxpayer and farmer as well as the
underdeveloped countries of the world. But the moral
obligation extends beyond simple pragmatics because it
emanates from the principles of justice and peace.

The United States has instituted anti-poverty programs to alleviate the misery of certain classes; now, this
same concept of social and economic balance and equal-
ization must be extended to whole countries. The world
is involved in a single revolutionary process of which
the first stage, the achievement of prosperity, has been

[4] See A. McCormack, ed., *Christian Responsibility and World Poverty* (Westminster, Md., 1963).

completed by the economically developed countries. These developed countries, however, now have an obligation to help the underdeveloped countries through this first stage of evolution.

> 162. It is true that surplus production of goods, especially in agriculture, can hurt a certain section of the population. Still, this does not mean that prosperous nations are exonerated from the obligation of extending emergency aid to the indigent and hungry. Rather, every ounce of ingenuity should be employed to cut down the unfavorable effects resulting from a surplus of goods and to distribute the burden equitably over the entire population.

Yet this aid must always be viewed for what it is: a temporary measure to relieve a difficult situation. Pride and justice would be desecrated if such economic aid continued for long periods of time. Individual contributions by nations are good and even obligatory in certain cases, but true charity and the respect for the dignity and personalities of men and nations demands the kind of help that leads to self-help. To help support a nation when it can help itself is a grave offense against justice because it is kept in a continuous state of infancy and dependency.[5] In this respect, paragraphs 161 and 162 of the encyclical have been rightfully subtitled "Emergency Aid."

II

To solve any problem permanently, it is necessary to discover the causes for its existence. This same rule applies to the alleviation and elimination of poverty

[5] Cf. F. M. Coffin, *Witness for Aid* (Boston, 1964), pp. 34–40.

throughout the world. When the United States, for example, sends food to starving people, this emergency aid may only do away with a symptom. Now, if the cause of this famine is only a momentary reversal—say, earthquake victims cut off from normal supply routes— the symptom and the cause will pass simultaneously. But if the cause of this famine is an inherent failure in a nation's ability to grow food, these food shipments may save many people from starvation temporarily, but the cause will remain. The Pope's demand that the rich countries come to the aid of the underdeveloped countries includes an element of symptomatic relief, but, ultimately, this aid must strike at causes. In short, all economic aid should finally help the underdeveloped countries help themselves.

In the West, one of the principal factors responsible for the elimination of poverty has been the application of technology to all human endeavors. The rapid and effective industrialization of the West was made possible through discoveries and inventions, and its prosperous economy continues to depend upon the development of improved technology. In the underdeveloped countries, however, these advances are lacking, and their economies will continue to be backward until the new technology is effectively applied.

163. In the case of many nations, nevertheless, emergency aid will not suffice to eliminate the permanent factors causing hunger and want. These derive for the most part from the primitive nature of an economy. The remedy for such situations cannot be found except by trying all possible approaches. A partial answer is to help the workers to acquire technical skills and professional compe-

tence. Another is to make available the capital needed to step up economic development with the help of modern methods and techniques.

The industrial breakthrough came with the application of technology. Through this application, each man could produce more, and the surplus revenues were returned as capital investments. Plants, foundries, factories expanded and improved. With fresh capital returned to industry, the resultant expansion put the economy into orbit as the new type of advanced, capitalized, industrialized, technological society of the West. This process was brought about by stringent savings and by the return of these savings into capital expansion and improvement. Since capital re-investment is the *sine qua non* of any industrialized society, without it a country becomes progressively poorer as its population and needs increase and its production falls further behind.

The peculiar development of Western industry has led to further problems. The West no longer has to depend on vast quantities of raw materials it formerly obtained from the underdeveloped countries of the world. By the use of synthetic fibers and chemicals, it has managed to produce the raw materials which were imported from other countries, especially from the underdeveloped countries. This development, of course, is making the rich countries richer and the poor countries poorer. As a remedy, the Pope stresses the need for technical and industrial aid in these countries so they can develop their own industrial and economic capacity in the shortest time possible. The poor nations must make this industrial revolution, and it can only be done with aid from the West.[6]

[6] Cf. B. Ward, *The Rich Nations and the Poor Nations* (New York, 1962), pp. 37–61.

If aid from the West does not come, these underdeveloped countries can easily drift toward totalitarianism, which promises rapid industrialization through the hard times of slave labor and absolute government control. The temptation is great, for Russia made its industrial breakthrough in forty years while it took the West over two hundred years. India, of course, is the crucial example. It is trying to make an industrial breakthrough while preserving democratic institutions. It cannot depend on its own capital economy because it is underdeveloped. Since the people are so poor, savings for investment are almost out of the question. If India is to avoid strict government ownership, the only remedy is aid from the more developed countries. The situation, however, should not pose itself as a mere threat of "Give or we will go communist"; it is a basic alternative to real needs in these countries of which India is only one example. In the United States, the low wages paid to 35 million immigrants furnished the surplus capital necessary for the industrial revolution. The Soviet Union paid a cruel price in the lives of millions and millions of uprooted and starved peasants. It was brief and ruthless, but it was successful. As a primary example, India presently wants to bring such a radical industrial revolution to a primitive society, and it wants to do so through democratic institutions, without recourse to coercion or to class warfare and hatred. If India fails and resorts to totalitarianism, the West shall have failed to make the world safe for freedom, no matter how great its nuclear fire power. If India succeeds, it will signal a definite turn in the history of the industrial revolution and will assure the survival of democratic freedom in over half of the world's population.

What the underdeveloped countries desperately need are skills, engineering tools, and factory equipment. They have more than enough manpower for two industrial revolutions. When wealthier countries supply technological assistance, manpower will be brought into reaction with resources at much lower social pressures; but without this aid, social pressures increase and lead to brutal revolutions and a rapid turning away from free and democratic institutions. Faced with such a situation, it is almost madness for the West to attempt to cut back its foreign aid programs. If anything, they must be increased on all levels. At least this is the mind of the Pope.

165. With such aims in view, world and regional organizations, individual states, foundations and private societies today are offering such countries generous help and greater technical cooperation in all spheres of production. They are assisting thousands of young people to study in the universities of more advanced countries and to acquire an up-to-date scientific and professional formation. Meanwhile world banking institutions, single states and private persons often furnish capital and thus make possible the rise of a network of economic enterprises in the underdeveloped nations.

We are happy to profit by the present occasion to express Our sincere appreciation of such generous plans. But it is Our hope that in the years ahead the wealthier nations will redouble their efforts to promote the scientific, technical and economic progress of the underdeveloped nations.

The urgent need for such aid has also been eloquently stated by Barbara Ward:

But I have the impression that when we talk so confidently of liberty, we are unaware of the awful servitudes that are created by the ancient enemies of mankind: the servitude of poverty when means are so small that there is literally no choice at all; the servitude of ignorance when there are no perspectives to which the mind can open because there is no education on which the mind can begin to work; the servitude of ill-health which means that the expectation of life is almost too short to allow for any experiences of freedom and the years that are lived and dragged out without the health and strength which are themselves a liberation.[7]

There can be no dignity, no freedom, and no human development in such situations. That is why the Pope always insists on the social nature of the causes and remedies of these problems, and why he always has before him the foundation of his letter—the promotion of the human dignity of man as God wills him to live in the world.

Yet both East and West have a temptation to "use" their aid as a method of promoting their own causes. The East, and particularly Russia, has its own form of colonialism, as in Eastern Europe, and does its best to foment revolutions in other nations. The West is not blameless. To show this blame, it is unnecessary to dig up the past abuses of Western imperialism and colonialism all over the globe; it is only necessary to read of CIA agents fomenting revolution in South Viet Nam and all of Latin America for supposedly "anti-communist" reasons.[8]

On the other hand, the Marshal Plan and the Alliance

[7] *Op. cit.*, p. 158.
[8] See some rather sordid reports of the CIA's activity in D. Wise and T. Ross, *The Invisible Government* (New York, 1964). Time gained by such activities can be effectively utilized only if those who have purchased it know what they want to do with it. This requires, under modern world conditions, a broadly shaped and reasonably progressive vision of the world they wish to create through the use of power. There are very few indications that such coherent vision is even beginning to come into being in Washington.

for Progress are steps in the right direction, so that, in the words of the late Mr. Kennedy, "the world may be free for diversity." As these programs show, aid must be given by respecting the cultural and moral traits of the people involved. And as *Pacem in terris* states so clearly, the richer nations must attempt to make the poorer capable of assuming their own destinies both politically and economically:

> 171. But the more highly developed nations face an even greater temptation. They must take care lest, while giving help to less developed nations, they turn the political situation that prevails there to their own profit or imperialistic aggrandizement.
>
> 172. If such an attempt be made, it must be explicitly labeled as an effort to introduce a new form of colonialism, which, however cleverly disguised, would be only a repetition of that old, outdated type from which many peoples have recently escaped. It would, too, have a harmful impact on international relations and constitute a threat to world peace.
>
> 173. Necessity and justice alike demand that technical and financial aid be given with sincere political disinterestedness and for the purpose of bringing those underdeveloped nations to the point where they can advance themselves economically and socially.
>
> 174. In this way, a precious contribution would be made to the formation of a world community, a community in which all members, aware of their duties and rights, strive on a basis of equality to achieve universal prosperity.

The fruition of such aid will result in all types of

political and economic diversity, because these poor nations must be free to choose how they wish to conduct their own destiny.

Mutual distrust of East and West remains. This distrust is evinced in their respective budgets for military expenses as compared to those for aid to poorer countries. Furthermore, this disproportion is distorted because the rich nations inflate their claims to the size of their foreign aid programs. A dispassionate estimate of the amount of foreign aid occurs in the 1962 report on the economic and social consequences of disarmament, which was prepared by an international group of expert consultants. The report indicates that the new flow of aid from rich to poor nations runs between 3.5 billion and 4 billion dollars per year. This U.N. report is corroborated by independent estimates which show that the total rate of investment in the underdeveloped countries does not exceed 20 billion dollars, or less than 20 percent of the amount spent for armaments by the rich countries. In foreign aid, the United States contributes 2 billion dollars (about 40% of the total), but this amounts to about $\frac{1}{16}$ of its military budget (51 billion).[9] Furthermore, American foreign aid represents an infinitesimal part of the 612 billion dollar gross national product of 1963. On the scale of dollars, vacations, costing 30 billion dollars, are 15 times more important for Americans than aid to literally millions of the world's poor. Thus the Pope concludes:

> 203. Individuals, and even all people, grow more and more convinced of this every day. Nevertheless, it seems that men, especially those entrusted with greater responsibility, are unable to

[9] The arms race is more broadly discussed in *Pacem in terris*, par. 109–119, and the reader is referred to that document for a more complete development of the subject.

achieve the understanding and co-operation which the general public ambitions.

The root of such inability is not to be sought in any shortage of scientific knowledge, technical skill or economic proficiency, but in the absence of mutual trust. Men, and consequently states, fear one another. Each fears that the other harbors plans of conquest and is cunningly waiting for the right moment to put these plans into effect. Hence, each organizes its own defenses and arms itself, so it says, to deter other nations from launching an invasion.

204. As a consequence, vast human energies and gigantic resources are employed for destructive rather than constructive purposes. Meanwhile, individuals and peoples suffer from an oppressive uneasiness that lessens the spirit of initiative for more significant undertakings.

One of the gravest problems of modern times is the so-called population explosion, or overpopulation. To a large degree, this rapid expansion in the population is due to the reduction in infant mortality by the introduction of modern medical and hygienic techniques. In certain countries, as in Latin America or India, these medicines and methods have all but nullified the economic growth made in the past few years. In India alone, the money necessary to support eight million new additions has eaten away the surplus capital needed for industrial expansion and, consequently, the economic growth of the whole country. The situation is practically the same in many of the underdeveloped countries. The Pope recognizes this situation when he sums up the problem of the population explosion in rather Malthusian terms:

187. It is clear that in the less developed nations —still relying on statistical data—the rapid spread of modern hygienic methods and medical remedies reduces the death rate among infants, and thus lengthens the lifespan. At the same time, the number of births, where it is now normally high, tends to remain more or less constant, at least for a considerable period of time. But, while the number of births exceeds the number of deaths in the same year, the productive efficiency of the respective economic systems does not increase proportionately. Accordingly, an improvement in the standard of living in these underdeveloped states is almost impossible. Indeed, it is rather inevitable that things will get worse. Hence, to avoid a situation which will result in extreme hardship, there are those who would have recourse to drastic measures of birth control or birth prevention.

In 1650 the population of the world did not exceed 500 million. By 1950, the population had grown to about 2½ billion; and in 1965, it was well over 3 billion human beings. In less than 14 years, from 1950 to 1964, the number added to the world's population was the same as the total population in 1650. At this rate of growth, by 2000 A.D. there will be some 6 billion people on the earth, and by the year 2600 A.D. there will scarcely be one square yard of land for each person on earth.

Demographers are in serious disagreement on the number of people the earth could support if all the resources presently known were fully employed. Their estimates range anywhere from 15 to 100 billion human beings. The Pope concludes that the scope of the problem as a whole is not at all certain:

188. The truth is that the relation between the

size of the world population and the available resources does not seem—at least for the moment and in the near future—to create a serious difficulty. For the elements from which one might draw conclusions on this question are too uncertain and controversial.

In his optimistic way, the Pope has confidence both in God's goodness and in the infinite possibilities of man's reason and ingenuity which have always found ways to cope with difficult situations.

189. Besides, God in His goodness and wisdom has implanted in nature inexhaustible resources and has endowed man with a sufficient measure of intelligence to create instruments fit to turn its products to the satisfaction of his needs and wants.

Hence, the real solution of the problem is not to be found in expedients that offend against the moral order established by God and do violence to the very origin of human life. It will be had, instead, from a renewed scientific and technical effort on the part of man to deepen and extend his mastery over nature. The progress of science and technology achieved to date opens up limitless horizons in this direction.

By and large, however, the problem of overpopulation remains on local levels, especially in the more underdeveloped countries.

190. We appreciate the fact that in certain underdeveloped areas and states serious problems and difficulties of this nature can and do present themselves. These problems frequently result from a defective economic and social organization which

does not provide means of subsistence in a measure proportionate to the rate of population increase, and also from the fact that a sense of solidarity among peoples is not operative to a sufficient degree.

All demographers agree that at present there is over population only in these specific areas. In these underdeveloped countries, much of this increase has been due to a decrease in infant mortality and to a prolongation of the lifespan. When a population is young, its death rate will be low and not proportionate to its birth rate. Almost one half of the persons living in Latin America are under the age of 25 because of the cut in infant mortality. Someday the birth and death rate will level off at a better ratio than at present, but the present problem is pressing.

As a solution to the problem of overpopulation, countries like Japan have undertaken massive government-supported programs of abortion, sterilization, and contraceptive birth control. Beyond doubt, this program has drastically curtailed the number of births. In Japan, the national birth rate plunged from 33.5 in 1948 to 21.5 in 1953 and to 17.2 in 1957, where it has since stabilized. Abortions in Japan have swelled to over a million a year, and many people believe that the true number of abortions is really about two million. This program, however, is now under serious reconsideration because of its predicted effect on business and on the future population. "Whereas there were six persons age 20–59 for every one person above age 60 in 1955, there will be only 2.1 persons in the working ages for 1 above age 60 in the year 2015. This foreshadows a labor shortage in Japan on a scale which has perhaps never been equaled in world history. Funds which are now being stored away by thrifty parents for old age may help them little if there are so few workers in the nation. Pensions, social security funds, life insurance and interest will lose value through excessive inflation."[10]

The Pope's program, however, is positive. He insists that men must attempt to remedy the population problem by applying all of the many technical resources available. Yet he does not exclude the fact that children must be brought into this world in a responsible way. The Pope clearly recognizes the obligation incumbent on married couples to train their children:

> 195. It is of the greatest importance that the younger generation be brought up with an adequate cultural and religious formation. Parents have the duty and right to see to this formation and to equip the young with a profound sense of responsibility in all life's deeds, including those connected with setting up a family and the conception and education of children. These children ought to be taught not only an abiding trust in Divine Providence, but also a resolute willingness to undergo inevitable fatigue and sacrifices in the fulfillment of a mission so noble and often so arduous as is the co-operation with God in the transmission of human life and the education of offspring. Toward such education no institution provides more efficacious help than the Church by its guidance and spiritual resources. For this reason, too, the Church's right to full liberty in fulfilling her mission must be recognized.

The Church has never advocated an unrestrained proliferation. Reason demands that married couples

[10] A. Zimmerman, "Birth Control in Japan" in *World Justice*, 5 (Sept., 1963), p. 50.

bring into this world only those children that they can socially, educationally and psychologically care for. The commandment is both to procreate and educate children. We have perhaps stressed the former at the cost of the latter, but now a better balance is required. When modern parents have to feed, dress, and educate their children on a limited or fixed income, the limitation of children, at least for the vast majority, is a basic necessity.

Through the ages, the Church has stressed one or another of her teachings because of the existence of positive error or of the danger of miscomprehension. Today, a serious understanding of modern industrial and economic society requires intelligence and courage, and this new type of society has made necessary an increased stress on the education of children. The obligation to increase cannot therefore negate the equal obligation to educate. Modern theologians have revealed that parenthood ought to be responsible within the framework of Christian prudence. The word *responsible* has to be understood in the Christian sense, not the neo-pagan sense. Materialists use the word *responsible* along with the word *planning*, and thus a man plans a family as he would plan a housing project or a factory. Seeing the destructiveness of "the iron law of wages," Karl Marx applied the concept of responsible planning of reproduction to fit economic needs. Some Catholics even concede that Marxian and Catholic ends are the same—that is, the limitation of offspring; but the present problem is to find a means ("the pill," for example) which will be acceptable to all religious groups. Such an understanding by a Christian clearly indicates that he misapprehends the meaning of the word *responsible* in the phrase "responsible parenthood."

Totally open to God and to His chosen in the sacred

act of marriage, the Christian approaches both with the generosity of heart and of gift which implies trust and confidence in God.

> 196. Genesis relates how God imposed on the first human beings two complementary commands: the first, *Increase and multiply;* the other, *Fill the earth and subdue it.*
>
> 197. Now certainly the divine command to dominate nature is not aimed at destructive purposes. Instead, it is directed to the betterment of human life.

The Christian does not approach these problems in the spirit of a calculating machine. Obviously, he must reflect and be prudent, taking into consideration the concrete situation as it presents himself to him, as God reveals it to him in the circumstances of his daily Christian experience.

> When a couple face the question whether they may or should desire a new addition to their family, Christian prudence permits them to see all the factors in the proper light and proportion, starting with health, daily bread, housing, right up to the question of education. Since prudence is a daughter of wisdom, a form of love, the crucial question is: Is the concrete desire for another child here and now a true expression of love of God, of love of spouse, of the love of the children already born, of love of the being whose existence is really at issue?[11]

The Christian's attitude toward "responsible parenthood" is first an act of faith, based on the firm belief that God is all-knowing and will communicate that knowl-

[11] B. Häring, *Commonweal,* 80 (June 5, 1964), p. 325.

edge; it is an act of hope, emanating from the knowledge that God will never abandon a man unless he abandons God first; and above all, it is an act of love, of charity, where *all* responsibilities are considered in the light of gift, of generosity, and of life. From this understanding, the Christian married couple can come to their own conclusion on what is the "ideal" number of children. Since God's will alone, sought by married couples in the openness of faith, determines the number of children in any family, this number will be the personal ideal of each Christian couple, and not that of their neighbors or even of the faithful in another country, whose circumstances are always unique. "True Christian prudence is involved in the specific question whether now, in given circumstances and as long as these circumstances obtain, any addition to the family should be sought."[12] In this sense, more praise is due to the good Protestant who is generous, open in faith and love, free in the gift of self, but uses contraceptives than to the calculating Catholic who sticks rigidly to the rhythm chart, but whose intention is vitiated by selfishness in not willing to be as generous as his concrete circumstances will allow. This distinction of praise does not imply that the means used to attain an end are unimportant, but simply that, in the final analysis, things such as ungenerous intentions can be more vicious.

At this point, the Christian concerned with the population explosion ought to be on his guard. While it may be true that Catholics have insisted too much on only one solution to the problems faced by the economically underdeveloped countries—namely, increasing food, production, industrialization, and so on—many other public and private groups, such as the planned parent-

[12] *Ibid.*, p. 326.

hood associations, have claimed that the poverty in these countries would soon pass if they only practiced birth control or sterilization. Catholics must not be deceived by this claim. To stem the world's poverty, birth limitation and an increase in foreign aid are both needed. Even if science were to make a breakthrough in some birth control technique acceptable to all or most religious groups, the problem of underdevelopment would remain, and it is a problem which requires ingenuity, good will, and imagination for its solution. Without some limit to the birth rate, however, the fruit of industrial progress is immediately eaten up by the basic needs of the many new mouths in the population. Last year, India created two million jobs with its new industries, but there was also an increase of eight million people in population. Over a long period of time, such a situation in an area of economic underdevelopment can only lead to disaster. More government funds ought certainly to be channeled into research on the reproductive cycle of humans. In spite of great advances in other fields of medicine, man's knowledge of sexology is, to say the least, very limited. Accurate knowledge of reproduction will further man's responsibility over this aspect of human nature.

In the present circumstances, however, Pope John XXIII prefers to recommend technical and industrial help as the immediate solution for underdeveloped countries of the world. From a global point of view, he does not as yet see a problem of overpopulation (par. 188), but this does not mean that he excludes such an eventuality. On the contrary, the tenor of paragraph 189 is that there might well be a real problem in the not so distant future, but the problem can be bridged when it becomes clear. In the underdeveloped countries, however, overpopulation often exists (par. 190), but the

Pope immediately adds that the situation cannot be remedied by those means which Catholic morality rejects—that is, artificial contraception, sterilization and abortion.

> 191. But even in such an hypothesis, We must immediately make clear, these problems should not be approached or solved by having recourse to methods and means which are unworthy of man and which are advocated by those who entertain an utterly materialistic conception of man and of human life.

This statement does not rule out serious study of reproduction in order to discover means which would not offend Catholic principles. If man is permitted to extend rationality over nature, then why not over his sexuality? The Pope, for his part, prefers not to go into detail on this problem because it is under close examination in the Church by serious theologians, bishops, and laymen. In an address as recent as June, 1964, Pope Paul VI stated that the use of steroids was under consideration by Church authorities and theologians.

Leaving this problem which still requires more study, Pope John concentrates on what can be done *now* for the poor of the world in conjunction with all men of good will:

> 192. In Our judgment this question can be solved only when the socio-economic betterment of both individuals and society as a whole respects and promotes true human values. In other words, the solution is to be found only in socio-economic progress achieved in a moral atmosphere befitting the dignity of mankind and the immense value of a single human life. Furthermore, it must also em-

brace world-wide co-operation that permits and favors an orderly and fruitful international exchange of useful knowledge, capital and manpower.

Such an effort must be international. No one country can solve this world problem, for, as the Pope states more fully in *Pacem in terris,* the human race is one in co-responsibility, in caring for one another. For the first time in history, man commands the technical knowledge to eliminate poverty from the earth, and no man or group of men need be enslaved by droughts, floods, erosion, and insects of all types. As the Aswan Dam in Egypt is demonstrating, man can reclaim whole deserts by the use of dams and irrigation. Man can tap the ocean depths for oil and minerals, as is being done by oil companies in the North Sea; he can harness the atom to drive his machinery, as is being done in atomic submarines and ships; he can launch rockets to explore the moon, as is being done by American and Russian rocketry; he can move mountains for roads and canals, as is presently being planned for Panama. All these means and methods are now at man's disposal.

The Pope next makes a fine point in human as well as national psychology. Aid can never be wholly disinterested. This is to deny the human condition. Paragraphs 171–172 ("Disinterested Aid") must be read with paragraph 202 to obtain the Pope's balanced view of the matter.

200. The relations among nations everywhere have lately multiplied and increased under the impact of science and technology. In turn, their populations necessarily become more and more interdependent.

201. As a result, it can be said that contemporary

problems of any importance, whatever their content may be—scientific, technical, economic, social,
political or cultural—today commonly present su-
pernational and often global dimensions.

202. Hence, individual nations can no longer
adequately solve their major problems in their own
environment and with their own resources. This is
true even in instances where they are communities
notable for the high level of their culture and
humaneness, for the number and industriousness of
their citizens, for the efficiency of their economic
systems and the vast size and richness of their
territories. Nations, indeed, must perforce supplement and develop one another. And it may be said
that each succeeds in developing itself by contributing to the development of the others. Hence,
mutual understanding and co-operation are a
prime necessity.

The nations of the world have become more interdependent on, not independent of, each other. Because of
rapid communications and a more diversified demand
for goods and raw materials, the economy of the world
is more international today than it has ever been in the
history of man. A country today must play its economic
role in closer relation to that of other countries. If the
1929 stock market crash in the United States shows how
the collapse of one economy can have an effect on the
whole world, the European Common Market illustrates
what prosperity individual nations can achieve through
international planning. The basic question is no longer
whether there is to be national and international "planning." This is simply a fact. The question today is planning for whom and for what (rich and poor nations).
If one country undersells another on the international

market, moreover, the whole balance of international payments is affected. This situation is becoming more apparent to individual nations in their trade agreements. The "Kennedy Round" of trade negotiations in 1964 is a good example of how aid to the economically underdeveloped countries can result in providing additional markets for the goods of the richer nations. Thus the three-month World Trade Conference at Geneva completed its work by signing a compromise agreement between rich and poor nations. In the agreement, a 55-member trade organization was established to help developing nations, thereby narrowing the economic gulf between the "have" and the "have-not" countries. In a concluding speech, Britain suggested a four-point aid program designed to assist the poor nations: an increase in the contribution to the United Nations technical assistance programs; support for an increase in the U.N. budget to expand its activities in industrial development; readiness to provide capital assistance to the African development bank; and sympathetic consideration of assistance to other regional development banks.

At one point, this 119-nation conference threatened to break down in discord over the developing countries' demand for a bigger share of aid and trade and the advanced nations' insistence on control of aid. Efforts to eliminate the discord culminated in a compromise which proposed a new international trade organization that would operate under the U.N. as "the trade and development board." The new organization will continue the work begun by the Geneva conference in helping underdeveloped countries toward economic and social betterment.

In a letter to the Vatican delegation to the Geneva trade talks, Pope Paul VI made some solid observations:

The Holy See has encouraged without reserve the various steps taken by the United Nations since the creation in 1949 of the Expanded Program of Technical Assistance, such as the Special Fund, the vast worldwide campaigns launched by the specialized agencies tackling some of the most urgent problems, and the continuous and improved endeavors to raise the standard of living and to combat certain evils which traditionally afflict a large portion of humanity.

These efforts are now increasing within the framework of the Decennial Development Plan, one of its first steps being the "United Nations conference on scientific and technical applications in underdeveloped countries" to which the Holy See sent an official delegation.[13]

The ethics of international responsibility are evident not only in the thought of Pope Paul, but throughout the social teachings of the Church. As Pope John made clear in *Pacem in terris,* all men are responsible for the world's poor.

III

The Pope does not fail to consider another problem which besets the underdeveloped countries of the world: often, there is a great distance between the various classes in the same country, some being fabulously rich while others are miserably poor.

54. It is obvious that recent advances in scientific knowledge and productive technology provide public authorities with far greater capacities than in the past for reducing inequalities among the various sectors of production, among

[13] Reported in *The Catholic Messenger,* 82 (July 16, 1964), p. 5.

the various areas within the same nation, and among the various peoples of the world.

This development also puts it within their competence to control fluctuations in the economy and to bring effective remedies to bear on the problem of mass unemployment. Consequently, those in authority responsible for the common good are more and more required to undertake a variety of economic activities, at once more vast and more highly organized. It is also essential for this purpose that they devise suitable structures, programs, means and methods. . . .

79. When one considers it on the national level, the common good demands the following: to provide employment to the greatest number of workers; to prevent the emergence of privileged classes even among the workers; to maintain an equal balance between wages and prices; to make goods and services of a higher quality available to the greatest possible number; to eliminate or check inequalities existing between the sectors of agriculture, manufacturing and services; to effect a balance between economic expansion and the development of essential public services; to adjust as far as possible the means of production to the progress of science and technology; finally, to insure that improvements in the standard of living should not only serve the interests of the present but also look to the advantage of future generations.

80. There are also demands of the common good in the international order: to avoid all forms of unfair competition between the economies of different countries; to encourage harmony, understanding and fruitful collaboration among these

national economies; to co-operate effectively in the economic development of underdeveloped nations.

There can be no doubt that within many countries of the world today there is a great disparity between the poverty-stricken many and the opulent few. Latin America immediately comes to mind. As a continent, it is one of the most destitute in the whole world, and this destitution extends to its moral fiber as well as its economy. By the year 2000 the population of Latin America will have doubled, and yet its present economic and industrial development is much too slow to keep pace with its exploding population. Agriculture is poor in methods as well as in produce and is not fulfilling the absolute needs of the present population. Due to a quasi-colonial status begun by the Spanish and other European and North American exploiters and continued by the Latin American oligarchs themselves, there is little variety in agricultural produce. In many cases, Latin American countries have a one-crop economy. This kind of economy gives them an unfavorable balance in international payments, making them bad credit risks. The wealth that does exist is fantastically divided: less than 20% of the Latin Americans own over 80% of the real estate and the liquid and capital assets.[14] This unjust distribution of wealth is further inflamed by an almost complete lack of a graduated income tax structure, that would put wealth and the ability to pay in some kind of equitable proportion. As a result of such inequitable ownership, there is woeful need of agrarian reform; the few own most of the land in Latin America,

[14] Gary McLoin, *Latin America: The Eleventh Hour* (New York, 1963).

while the many are poor sharecroppers leading a sub-human existence.[15] The cities are rapidly becoming the focus of population, but they have been built in a haphazard and planless way, producing some of the worst slums in the entire world. All these difficulties are coupled with poor labor organization, illiteracy on a mass scale, and the absence of any training and participation in political democracy. Indeed, with the absence of economic democracy, political democracy is an ironic mockery.

Essentially, Latin America needs a complete revolution in its social structure, and, without it, there can be no freedom, no peace, and no justice. In Brazil, for instance, 80% of all irrigable and workable lands are owned by 2% of the population. The gross injustice of such a regime can be counterbalanced only by a sane program of agrarian reform which is at once just and practical. The so-called "lazy" Mexican does not sleep most of the day because he has no ambition; he does so because he is ridden with various diseases and worms, which make sleep his only sedative. It has been shown more than once that if these people are given some hope, enough to eat, decent housing, and medical help, they can produce as much as or more than their well-fed North American counterparts.

In these countries, however, there is a great difference between the poverty of today and the poverty of former times.[16] Today there is a "revolution of rising expectations" throughout the world, and even the most illiterate know that they need not remain in poverty—that there is a way out. Whether it comes from the West or the East, there is hope. If a revolution in these unjust

---

[15] R. Katzenstein, "Feudal Capitalism Strangles the Progress of Latin America" in *Social Order*, 12 (June, 1963), pp. 5–12.

[16] United Nations, *The UN Development Arcade: Proposals for Action* (New York, 1962), p. 12.

social conditions cannot come about by justice and peace under law, then it will certainly come about by violent revolution and war in spite of blockades, in spite of armies supported by the rich, and in spite of ideologies. The social revolution is a flood which cannot be stopped; it can only be channeled. Whether it comes through democratic regimes or through totalitarianism and communism is a matter which can be settled only by the richer countries which recognize the fundamental justice of these claims and give help accordingly. This technical and industrial assistance must be used in such a way that, under the principle of subsidiarity, these people are encouraged to help themselves through their own initiative. As the Pope repeats so often in *Mater et Magistra,* any aid given by foreign governments or by the domestic government should encourage and help citizens take on their own responsibility and development. India and Latin America have huge populations for use in industry, but they must first be well-fed and well-trained before they can put this great potential to work. Foreign aid is therefore a basic catalyst for uniting men with materials to produce a modern industrialized society. It is indeed a crude form of aid which keeps people completely dependent on doles; it denies man the ability to be himself, to develop his potentialities and abilities.[17] Aid, then, must be directed to help the masses of people help themselves, through training, education, and organization.

In Latin America there are three principal enemies of social progress and expectation. The first of these enemies is the governments, which, for the most part, are dictatorships of either the right or the left, but mainly of the right. Totalitarian in nature, their great excuse for

[17] R. V. Carrasco, "The Problems in Latin America" in *World Justice,* 5 (September, 1963), p. 60.

not initiating greater social reforms is the communist
threat against which they are the bastions. They perpetuate a *status quo* which is nothing more than a protection of the few rich against the just expectation of the
very many poor. Any foreign aid which supports these
disgraceful conditions under the guise of combating
communism will lose the war in the long run even if it
gains small victories in the short run.

The second enemy of Latin American social progress
is the existence of a wealthy few. Like all the rich, they
are reluctant to give up their privileges of wealth and
power and make sacrifices for the common good. Much
of the wealth produced in Latin America is not re-
invested in capital expansion for the benefit of the total
community; it is shipped out of the country to Switzer-
land or to secret accounts on Wall Street, thereby destroying indigenous economic expansion. Their attitude
towards social reform, like that of their government, is
confined to directing anti-communist propaganda
against anyone or any group, including missionaries,
that demands social reform. Their status and privileges
will decline and be redistributed, but the only real
question is how. Will they realize their responsibilities
and contribute to this common effort, or will they wait
for violent overthrow? As Mr. Kennedy said so well:
"No amount of external resources, no stabilization of
commodity prices, no new inter-American institutions
can bring progress to nations which do not have political stability and determined leadership. No series of
hemispheric agreements or elaborate machinery can
help those who lack internal discipline, who are unwilling to make sacrifices and renounce privileges. No one
who sends his money abroad, who is unwilling to invest
in the future of his own country, can blame others for

the deluge which threatens to overwhelm them."[18]

Finally, communism poses one of the most formidable threats to a just social society in Latin America. Given the situation of social and economic stagnation and selfishness, the appeal of communism grows daily more attractive as a way, and perhaps the only way, out of these terrible social, cultural, and economic conditions. Ranting and raving about the superiority of political democracy is a waste of time unless it is accompanied by a willingness to develop an economic democracy, for, without it, the communists are bound to foment a struggle. The only real choice in Latin America is between Marxism and a socially enlightened Christianity, which alone can promote man's material welfare and his human dignity.

As long as there is no way out of the present dilemma, communism will continue to win over countless millions of peasants as well as dissatisfied intellectuals. Catholics in particular must be more and better trained in the social teaching of the Church and in concrete action; they must apply it to the particular situations in their own countries. It comes as a deep shock to note that the reactionary few in Latin America are Catholics who simply cannot or will not see their grave moral obligation to make sacrifices for the social reconstruction of their countries. If Catholics teach human values and dignity to these people in the schools and in literature, and yet offer them no way to achieve these basic values in their daily lives, then, in reality, Catholics are preparing the way for revolution and rebellion against the existing decadent social order and, ironically, they are helping the communists exploit the unjust condition

[18] A. Nevins, ed. *The Burden and the Glory* (New York, 1964), p. 161.

between the ideal of man and his actual existence. If *Mater et Magistra* were fully implemented and not merely preached by Catholics, communism would not have the proverbial leg to stand on in Latin America.

The United States has endeavored to meet the Latin American challenge on its own ground. Americans have recognized that aid, if it is to be effective, must finally permit people to help themselves. Channeled through the Alliance for Progress, American aid is based on the concept of social reform in all sectors. In this sense, the *Allianza* is invaluable from two points of view. Its direct object is not just aid (even though there is 2.5 billion dollars worth), but social reconstruction and development. By demanding that the domestic governments match United States aid dollar for dollar, the Latin American countries must seriously consider the possibility of a graduated income tax reform, which is a basic necessity for a just society. Secondly, and this point has not as yet received the stress it should have, co-operation with private groups, both secular and religious, implements reform much better than giving wholesale aid to sometimes beaurocratic governments whose corruption is well-known. This kind of co-operation has the added advantage of going to the roots of the problem: the betterment of the vast majority of poor Latin Americans. Mr. Kennedy expressed it well:

And if we are successful—if our effort is bold enough and determined enough—then the close of this decade will mark the beginning of a new era in the American experience. The living standards of every American family will be on the rise—basic education will be available to all—hunger will be a forgotten experience—the need for massive outside help will have passed—most nations will have entered a period of self-sustaining growth—and, although there will still be much to do, every American republic will be the master of its own revolution of hope and progress.

Let me stress that only the determined efforts of the American nations themselves can bring success to this effort. They, and they alone, can mobilize their resources—enlist the energies of their people —and modify their social patterns so that all, and not just a privileged few, share in the fruits of growth. If this effort is made, then outside assistance will give a vital impetus to progress; without it, no amount of help will advance the welfare of the people.

Thus if the countries of Latin America are ready to do their part—as I am sure they are—then I believe that the United States for its part, should help provide resources of a scope and magnitude sufficient to make this bold development program a success, just as we helped provide resources adequate to help rebuild the economies of Western Europe. For only an effort of towering dimension can ensure fulfillment of our play for a decade of progress.[19]

IV

The United States is not exempt from depressed social conditions which the Pope warns against. Inside the United States are some 40 million Americans who do not share in the abundance of the American dream. But for the most part, they are hidden from the sight of the more affluent. While conditions in the slums of northern cities, in Appalachia, and among the aged and the Negroes are not as bad as those which exist in parts of

[19] Vital Speeches, 27 (April 1, 1961), p. 355.

Asia and Latin America, this certainly is no cause for comfort. Once out of the destitution stage, poverty is a matter of degree which can be measured against the prosperity surrounding it. This contrast must be the criterion in America. The average Negro baby born today has about one-half as much chance of completing high school as a white baby; one-third as much chance of being a professional man; twice as much chance of being unemployed. His wage earnings will be one-half those of a white baby, and he can expect to live seven years less than the white baby. The Negro is only one example from among the many poor of our society. There are many more: the aged, the Mexicans, the Puerto Ricans, and the "Wetbacks," to mention only the more conspicuous. "Here is the most familiar version of social blindness: 'The poor are that way because they are afraid of work. And anyway they all have big cars. If they were all like me, they could pay their way. But they prefer to live on the dole and cheat the taxpayers . . .' But the real explanation of why the poor are where they are is that they made the mistake of being born to the wrong parents, in the wrong section of the country, in the wrong industry, or in the wrong racial or ethnic group."[20]

At this time, it is unnecessary to discuss all of the social conditions of these other Americans. Many books have already been written about them, describing the social conditions and causes of this type of poverty.[21] Suffice it to say the so-called "war on poverty," if it works and if it is not a political gimmick, is today one of the most potent forces for bringing equality with dignity to millions of Americans who otherwise would continue to exist under the submarginal standards of living and

[20] M. Harrington, *The Other America* (New York, 1962), pp. 14–15.
[21] B. H. Bagdinkan, *In the Midst of Plenty* (Boston, 1964).

social conditions to which the affluent society of the sixties has relegated them.

As in the case of Latin America, a solution to American poverty presupposes a change in the basic social structures and in the economic sphere. The nation rightly applauded the passage of the most extensive civil rights bill since the Reconstruction, but that legislation will amount to nothing until the unskilled and untrained can gain the skill and training which will permit them to participate in the advanced industrialized society of America. Discrimination is certainly a potent factor in preventing certain groups from a full participation in American society, but the structural inability of the Negro and other minority groups to participate in American society is also a basic factor. Civil rights will mean little if a Negro or Puerto-Rican or poor white does not have the education he needs to participate actively in the American dream. They enjoy neither security nor a decent standard of living because of their structural situation; that is, they do not have the education and training to contribute actively and creatively to the economy. For the most part, these groups are faced with massive unemployment and slums (a euphemism for the homes of the poor) and a defeatist attitude in themsleves and their families. When a man is out of work for long periods of time through no fault of his own, he becomes apathetic and discouraged.[22]

After civil liberties have become an accepted fact in the United States, the Negro (and other minority groups) will still face a staggering difficulty to which Negro leadership has failed to give concerted thought: How will the Negro achieve economic liberty? Granted civil rights, there remains the horrendous fact that many

[22] See "Poverty U.S.A." in *Newsweek* (February 17, 1964), pp. 19–38.

Negroes simply lack the fundamental education and training to participate in the American economic and social structure. In a sense, this is a more formidable obstacle than civil rights themselves. In America, the individual's economic prosperity is an iron necessity without which he cannot possibly hope to penetrate into the American dream. Civil rights may end discrimination in restaurants, but what good will it do the Negro who is too poor to eat there anyway? The bill will end discrimination in employment, but if the Negro is unemployable because he lacks education and training, what good will it do him? American concern for the Negro must now pass beyond civil rights; it must move from racial integration to economic integration. A cynic once remarked that in America the bridge between the whites and the blacks is painted money green. There is much truth in this statement. Furthermore, in the interest of society, unemployment and unemployables are a great burden and necessitate costly welfare programs. This does not mean that through less welfare, human beings can be made more productive and responsible; it only means that money can be spent in a way that would be much better for the dignity of human beings as well as the taxpayers. For example, the comparatively small amount of public funds used to finance programs of retraining or adult education will save the taxpayer thousands of dollars in reduced public welfare loads.

The problem of eliminating poverty belongs primarily to the public authorities, state and federal. To refuse federal assistance, moreover, is to court the failure of any anti-poverty program; the federal government alone has the distributive funds for the job. Housing and slums are a perfect case in point. Time and again, private builders and local governments have proven themselves inadequate to the job. In 1961, Leon Keyserling, former Chairman of the President's Council of Economic Advisors, claimed that any serious attempt to eliminate slums would require two million new housing units per year for the next four years. The expenses incurred by such large-scale construction can only be met by a co-operation of local and federal authorities, a vital co-operation if poverty in the slums is to be conquered.[23] This venture will be expensive, costing possibly five to ten billion dollars a year for the next ten years. In the long run, however, this amount will pay itself over and over again through reduced crime and frustration and through increased productiveness in men and women. These reclaimed human beings will contribute a richness of their own to society through their talents and abilities, and, rewarded for their contribution, they will expand the consumer market for goods produced in the United States. A larger market means a greater consumption of goods, increased productions, and thus an expanding economy.

Most of structural unemployment in the United States is a result of a rapidly changing society. Progress in technology has been so rapid that whole sectors of the working population have been replaced. We have already seen that the modern techniques of farming have led to a rapid decrease in the number of farmers. As industry becomes more automated to meet the rising competition at home and from abroad, the number of workers will become smaller. The white-collar worker is no exception, since electronic computer machines are rapidly replacing him. In five or ten years' time, there will be practically no demand for the services of unskilled workers; and if present trends continue, jobs for semi-skilled workers are also in grave danger of extinction. More and more job opportunities will go only to

[23] M. Harrington, *op. cit.*, p. 154.

those who are highly educated and trained in technical work.

Palliatives such as the shorter work week, prolonged vacations, and early pensions are just that: palliatives for a situation which is endemic to the social structure itself. To have full employment, efforts must be directed towards meeting the demands of a highly technical modern society. Curiously enough, the present situation is ironic because there are not enough properly trained workers to meet demands and thus to expand the economy.[24] And yet there are millions of workers unemployed. Furthermore, the situation can only become worse with progress in technology and electronic computers. In other words, the labor market is glutted with the wrong kind of workers: this is what economists mean when they say that the poor are poor because of structural unemployment. Any youngster today who enters the labor force without technical training or an applicable trade is doomed to a life of unemployment and frustration. The employment situation became even more strained by 1965, when 4 million Americans reached the age of 18 and, consequently, overwhelmed the labor market. In 1950 only two million people had to be absorbed by the labor market.

In a condition of massive unemployment in which many persons are unemployable, there is stagnation in the economy, a great drain on public funds for welfare, and the manifold social evils of crime, slums, apathy, and discouragement. To reintroduce these millions of poor into the main stream of American life, training, retraining, education, price stability, urban renewal, and tax cuts are all important means in the war on poverty. In these ways, these people can attain the

[24] G. Myrdal, *Challenge to Affluence* (New York, 1963), Ch. 4–5.

personal responsibility and knowledge for ending their woes and a sense of dignity and purpose in society. The time when a man could lift himself up by his bootstraps and succeed in the economic world is almost gone; society has become so specialized and technical that, without a sound education and an applicable trade, a man simply cannot expect to succeed. He remains poor, not because he is lazy or shiftless, but because he does not have the ability to participate in the economy.

Public authorities have an obligation to provide the necessary programs for re-education. In this way, the hopelessly unemployed and unemployable will once again become productive citizens of society. Five to six percent of all unemployed Americans are structurally unemployed, and no amount of business expansion can remedy the situation. "This structural character of unemployment in America, means first that already at the present low rate of economic growth and the high and rising level of unemployment there is a scarcity of highly educated and skilled labor which shows up in the high figures for overtime by employees belonging to that elite . . . A balanced employment situation cannot be achieved simply by business expansion."[25] Any society which tolerates this kind of unemployment must be prepared to pay an exorbitant price in public welfare (now well over $65 billion a year), in police protection and in increasing crime rates and misfits of all kinds. Youth without channels to direct its energy constructively will direct it destructively. It is not by chance that the highest crime rates (rapidly increasing in all parts of the country) are among the unemployed in slums; the crime rate is proportionate to the unemployment rate. It makes no sense to construct new housing units if the

[25] G. Myrdal, *op. cit.*, p. 22.

slum psychology and unemployment are to follow. Increasing welfare payments, laudable in itself, cannot solve the structural difficulty.

The biggest drawback of poverty is that the poor have no organized political voice. Because they are poor, they have very little to offer the power politician; even their voting power is shrunk mainly because, being apathetic, they do not vote. They are largely silent, unheard from, and invisible. Unless the nation is willing to make a moral commitment to this sector of society, nothing will be done. The facts are undeniable: "Tens of millions of Americans are, at this very moment, maimed in body and spirit, existing at levels beneath those necessary for human decency. If these people are not starving, they are hungry, and without adequate housing and education and medical care. . . . This poverty twists and deforms the spirit. The American poor are pessimistic and defeated, and they are victimized by a mental suffering to a degree unknown in Surburbia."[26] Poverty in the midst of plenty gives the American much food for thought and action. Public effort must be concentrated in an effort to make society more humane for all of its members, and to do this, a massive public commitment of financial and personal resources is imperative.

There are also other forms of poverty of a non-material nature which should be attacked and eliminated if the national community is to reach its ultimate goals. As America becomes more urbanized and suburbanized, streams and lakes become more polluted by untreated sewage, industrial waste, and detergents which keep sudsing. The air itself is suffused with lung-rotting waste. Untended, air and water pollution destroys America's natural beauty and endangers the health of citizens. To know the immediacy of the problem, it is

[26] Harrington, *op. cit.*, p. 2.

only necessary to remember that Lake Erie will become another Dead Sea unless something is done to stem this tide of corruption. Furthermore, the problem of mass transportation and traffic congestion in large cities is becoming more acute. As American society becomes more affluent and two cars in every garage becomes the standard, the now congested streets of American cities will be unpassable. With the increase of motor vehicles, moreover, air pollution also increases. The proliferation of motor transportation has also contributed to the destruction, or at least the hiding, of natural beauty: if there is natural beauty to be seen along the nation's highways, billboard advertisers have done their best to hide it. Finally, the unwholesome poverty which pervades American cultural media, especially television and the cinema, is as appalling as it is unnecessary. The impoverishment of mind and taste can be as important as that of the body, and, in America, the talent to eliminate this poverty exists, but is not sufficiently encouraged.

Admittedly, the above problems will not cause men to die in the streets from starvation, yet their solution is necessary if man is to reach his full personal development.[27] And if Americans are truly concerned with their loss of individual initiative, these are as wide open for individual participation. When certain national politicians state unequivocally that Americans have lost the spirit of individualism, they unvariably point to the economic sphere as the proof. Even if this were true—and it is not—the example they cite to prove their claim shows the narrowness of their vision and the limit of their understanding of the American dream. The American dream concerns the whole man, and if a man becomes rich, it is still unfulfilled. In a broader vision of

[27] See *Pacem in terris,* par. 5–18.

the American dream, individualism can assert itself through public concern in attacking pollution of all kinds, through aesthetic concern in striving to preserve America the beautiful, and through spiritual concern in demanding the greatest cultural achievements of the Western world.

V

In his discussion of poverty, the Holy Father's endeavor is to awaken all nations to the needs of the poor, nationally and above all internationally. The emphasis in this encyclical, and in *Pacem in terris,* is brought to bear primarily on international poverty. The remarks are almost identical in both documents: the rights of the poor and the common destiny of this world's goods make the obligation of justice incumbent on all men of good will:

> 158. Mindful of Our role of Universal Father, We feel obliged to repeat solemnly what We have stated elsewhere: We are all equally responsible for the undernourished peoples. . . . [Therefore] it is necessary to awaken men's consciences to a sense of the responsibility which weighs upon everyone, especially upon those who are more richly blessed with this world's goods.

In a most special way, the Pope reminds Catholics that the Mystical Body of Christ has no boundries, makes no distinction of race, color or national origin. All men are truly brothers and sisters in the Kingdom of God in Christ, and this reality cannot be gainsaid by any type of political or economic prejudices:

> 159. It is obvious and the Church has always made it perfectly clear that the obligation to help

the poor and suffering ought to be felt most strongly by Catholics, in view of the fact that they are members of Christ's Mystical Body. John, the Apostle, said: *In this we have come to know His love, that He laid down His life for us, and we likewise ought to lay down our life for the brethren. He who has the goods of this world and sees his brother in need and closes his heart to him, how does the love of God abide in him?*

In both of these paragraphs, addressed as they are to Catholics and to all men of good will, the Pope appeals in the name of humanity and for humanity. Because of his pastoral concern, Pope John wishes to avoid strident commands and the appearance of strict juridical obligation. His is a plea from a father who appeals to his children to be mindful of their brothers in the human race and in the Mystical Body of Christ.

The Pope gives no doctrinaire ways and means of putting an end to poverty (par. 192). He states the moral problem and its urgency; he leaves the practical implementation to men of good will who are more able than he to accomplish this end. He asks that their aid be free from partisan political persuasions (par. 171); he also asks that it be increased on all levels, while praising what has already been done (par. 156, 164–165):

165. With such aims in view, world and regional organizations, individual states, foundations and private societies today are offering such countries generous help and greater technical cooperation in all spheres of production. They are assisting thousands of young people to study in the universities of more advanced countries and to acquire an up-to-date scientific and professional formation. Meanwhile world banking institutions, single states

and private persons often furnish capital and thus make possible the rise of a network of economic enterprises in the underdeveloped nations.

We are happy to profit by the present occasion to express Our sincere appreciation of such generous plans. But it is Our hope that in the years ahead the wealthier nations will redouble their efforts to promote the scientific, technical and economic progress of the underdeveloped nations.

The means to this end are varied: immigration and emigration, international banks and credit unions, technicians and businessmen in a type of peace corps, educators and teachers as papal volunteers, the Peace Corps, low interest loans and outright grants, public and private scholarships to universities in developed countries, equitable trade agreements favoring the underdeveloped countries, price stablization and international labor organizations. All these means and many others can be beneficial ways of aiding the economically underdeveloped nations. They must all be used in this concentrated international effort.

Before closing this section, the Pope has a special note of warning in regard to the hierarchy of values. There can be little doubt that the Pope is second to none in advocating a progressive and just social order within which men can live in material dignity and peace. The whole letter proves this point, and it is not necessary to repeat what is evident. But the material part of man is not the only part, nor even the most important. A man needs economic dignity: without it the vast majority of men are hardly able to give glory to God in a fitting way. Poverty is not a disgrace in itself, for disgrace means moral responsibility and the poor have usually had no part in their being poor. It is, however, an abnormal condition, an indirect result of original sin and, as such, is to be striven against with all the abilities man can master. But with every good there is a corresponding danger, and it is a wise man who can measure a good thing so that it does not absorb him completely.

175. Scientific and technical progress, economic development and the betterment of living conditions, if they occur together, certainly represent a positive contribution to human civilization. But we must realize fully that they are not the supreme values; for in comparison with the latter they are seen to be essentially instrumental in character.

176. We observe with sadness that many people in the economically advanced countries have no concern for a genuine hierarchy of values. These persons wholly neglect, put aside or flatly deny the existence of spiritual values. Meanwhile they energetically pursue scientific and technological research and seek economic development. Material well-being is in many instances their chief goal in life. This constitutes an insidious poisoning of the aid which economically advanced peoples can give to the underprivileged, in whom ancient tradition has often preserved a living and operative consciousness of the most important values at the base of human culture.

177. To undermine this consciousness is essentially immoral. One must respect it and, where possible, develop and refine it so that it will remain what it is: a foundation for true civilization.

Material advantage is for man, not man for material advantage. Without expounding the obvious, the search for material betterment can so absorb a man's mind and heart that he can forget that they are means to an end. From the gospels, it is clear that if a rich man is to get to heaven, it will depend upon how he used these gifts for the betterment of his brothers. The "American way of life," for example, is sometimes an euphemism for a crass and tawdry materialism. A distorted image of this "American way of life" has been successfully promoted by the movie industry, which features its type of sex, sadism, and, in general, a sordid materialism. Other nations can be and are adversely affected by such propaganda from the most prosperous nation on earth. Are we to identify America with this image abroad? Other nations have a right to the true image of what makes the United States a great nation: the Constitution, the Bill of Rights, and the sacred position and dignity of the individual. If America exports such materialistic notions, it is in grave danger of weakening the effect of its traditional moral and cultural values on others. The West's invasion into one of the most sacred areas of human life—sexual dynamism—also fits into this category. Brutal forms of birth control, sterilization, and abortion have been increasing in various Asiatic countries such as Japan and India. All of the consequences on the traditional moral and cultural values of these people have not as yet been calculated, but there is little doubt that if the dire consequences which are already appearing take full effect, the result will not be good for the West.

To conclude our analysis, the Pope makes his recommendations on the level of the international common good. The human family is one and, therefore, individual nations cannot escape their grave social responsibilities by hiding behind national boundaries. The universal common good is of monumental importance, and, as the Pope states in *Pacem in terris,*

98. Because relations between states must be regulated by the norms of truth and justice, they should also derive great benefits from active solidarity, through mutual co-operation on various levels, such as, in our own times, has already taken place with laudable results in the economic, social, political, educational, health and sport spheres. We must remember that of its very nature, civil authority exists, not to confine its people within the boundaries of their nation, but rather to protect, above all else, the common good of that particular civil society, which certainly cannot be divorced from the common good of the entire human family.

CHAPTER SIX

The Spiritual
and Temporal Task

I

THE LAST PART of *Mater et Magistra* is perhaps the most promising pontifical consideration of the human task here on earth in its relationship to the Kingdom of God. It could happily be called a chapter on Christian humanism built along the lines of Maritain's and Teilhard de Chardin's thought, except that the Pope does not adopt either of these views. Nonetheless the emphasis on the religious meaning of the layman's temporal task, although not an innovation, still takes on a greater intensity; unlike Pius XII, who also considered the layman's task, Pope John incorporates his observations and suggestions in a social encyclical, thereby showing the relationship of the layman's task to the social teaching of the Church. Though it is an integral part of the social teaching itself, it is, more specifically, the logical and practical application of the theoretical part of that teaching. For the first time in a pontifical document on the social order, a strong emphasis on action has been made an integral part of the Church's social thought. And because of this emphasis on the lay apostolate, this encyclical has rightly been called the encyclical of social Christian humanism. In another sense, it is also the encyclical that reveals the deep meaning of the lay apostolate in and for the world: the lay apostolate is not to convert the world from the outside, but it is to penetrate the world from within by understanding and accommodating Christian teaching to it. As Pope John pointed out in his address to the assembled Council Fathers on October 11, 1962, accommodation does not mean changing Catholic dogma. It means, instead, that Christians have the grave obligation to understand what the modern world is doing and where it is endeavoring to go; to see its great potential for good and to adapt Christian teaching to its particular mentality and genius; and by such application, to give it a deeply Christian direction and meaning.

In that address, the Pope showed the same qualities which he shows here with regard to the modern world: optimism, accommodation, understanding, approachability on both sides, goodness, and universalism. In both of his social documents, the Pope rules against the "prophets of doom" who can see nothing in the modern world except danger and temptation. The Pope admits that there is often grave danger which threatens the loss of everything; but he immediately reminds man that when the dangers are great, the possibilities for good are correspondingly great. Mankind might well be in moral danger of total annihilation by "the bomb"; but, through this same dangerous technology, he is on the threshold of overcoming some of the worst scourges of man: famine, disease, discrimination, space, and time. Mankind has entered the era of interplanetary space exploration; the economic interdependency of all nations is already achieved; nuclear energy promises an era of unprecedented expectation either for the total annihilation of the human race or for a progress unknown in the history of man; the need for international justice is at least theoretically recognized by all nations. The Church's response to this emerging world community must be one of hope and help. As the Pope points out so clearly, material and technical progress is a positive good but, by itself, it cannot really free man; and as history is showing, left to itself, material and technical progress gravely endangers the life of man on this planet because it has no spiritual nucleus or direction.

215. Wherefore, whatever the progress in technology and economic life, there can be neither justice nor peace in the world, so long as men fail to realize how great is their dignity; for they have been created by God and are His children. We speak of God, who must be regarded as the first and final cause of all things He has created. Separated from God, man becomes monstrous to himself and others. Consequently, mutual relationships between men absolutely require a right ordering of the human conscience in relation to God, the source of all truth, justice, and love.

217. However, no folly is more characteristic of the modern era than the absurd attempt to reconstruct a solid and prosperous temporal order while prescinding from God, the only foundation on which it can endure. It is equally foolish to seek to exalt man's greatness by drying up the font from which his greatness springs and from which it is nourished; that is, by restraining and, if possible, checking his quest for God. Daily events, which bring bitter disillusionment to many and even bloodshed to others, support the truth of the statement: *Unless the Lord build the house, they labor in vain that build it.*

Communism and other totalitarian ideologies which infest today's world can only lead man to self-destruction because they fail to recognize the sacred position of the individual human being, the core of any sane society. They, in effect, have a wrong view of the temporal because they consider it an end in itself. They do not or will not direct social progress as a means of achieving the dignity of the human person, towards whom the whole of the social order is geared and oriented.

II

In his general analysis of the ideological situation of the modern world, the Pope studiously avoids oversimplification. He notes with bitterness that there are persecutions of Christians in various parts of the world on both sides of the iron curtain, in such places as Ceylon and the Sudan as well as Russia. He might also have had in mind the persecutions of Orthodox communities in the Near East: for instance, the Armenians, among whom he was Apostolic Delegate for so long.

> 216. It is well known that for decades many of Our dearly beloved brothers and sons have suffered a ruthless persecution in many countries— including some with an ancient heritage of Christian civilization. This unhappy fact reveals to the eyes of the world the superior dignity of the persecuted in contrast to the cultivated barbarity of the persecutors. Even if it does not lead the latter to repentance, it does stir many men to deep reflection.

The Pope, however, is circumspect. He knows human history: men are never as good or as bad as the doctrines they preach, and ideologies do change during the process and under the pressures of human history and affairs:

213. In the modern era, different ideologies have been devised and spread abroad with this in mind. Some have already been dissolved as clouds by the sun. Others have undergone profound changes. In the case of still others, their hold on the minds of men today grows steadily weaker. And all this follows from the fact that they are ideologies which take into account only certain aspects of man, and these the less significant. Moreover, they overlook certain inevitable human imperfections, such as sickness and suffering, which even the most highly organized socio-economic systems obviously cannot totally remedy. Then there is that profound and imperishable religious instinct which stirs the hearts of men everywhere and which cannot be stamped out by violence or smothered by cunning.

The "certain aspects of man" are surely the material and economic, which are elevated at the cost of the spiritual. This elevation is clearly an error, but is it not possible that such doctrines will change when their errors become apparent? This modification was certainly the case with much of the nineteenth- and early twentieth-century socialism on the continent and in England. Its anti-spiritual and anti-clerical bias has all but disappeared, and its aims are now of a purely secular nature.

But how is the Christian to face these philosophic changes? What is he to do? A kind of co-existence was continued and formulated clearly in *Pacem in terris,* where the Pope said:

159. It must be borne in mind, furthermore, that

neither can false philosophical teachings regarding the nature, origin, and destiny of the universe and of man, be identified with historical movements that have social, cultural or political ends, not even when these movements have originated from those teachings and have drawn and still draw inspiration therefrom.

For these teachings, once they are drawn up and defined, remain always the same, while the movements, working on historical situations in constant evolution, cannot but be influenced by these latter and cannot avoid, therefore, being subject to changes, even of a profound nature. Besides, who can deny that those movements, insofar as they conform to the dictates of right reason and are interpreters of the lawful aspirations of the human person, contain elements that are positive and deserving of approval?

Among the many dramatic innovations of Pope John XXIII, his "opening to the left" held out the hope of a dialogue between the Church and communism. His willingness in *Pacem in terris* to recognize the impact of historical change on communist ideology and practice; his studious avoidance of inflamatory language when alluding to communism in all of his talks and encyclicals; his personal meeting with Khrushchev's son-in-law —all of these things represented a healthy departure from the earlier practice of the Church. Pope John understood that communism could change and, if it did, he wanted the Church to fill any vacuum left by that change.

Many Catholics were not happy with this turn of events, and a few even saw evidence that the "international left" had made its impact on the Vatican itself.

Through the voice of Will Herberg, the *National Review* was very disturbed at finding nothing in *Mater et Magistra* (or *Pacem in terris*) that further condemned communism. Pope John's silence on this aspect of today's world is significant, and that significance is found in the texts of both encyclicals. In *Pacem in terris,* the Pope points out that the order of peace is not merely the absence of war, as many think; it is not a "complete victory" over communism. The *order* of peace is founded on the *basis* of peace, which he exposes in the first two sections of the encyclical; it is founded on truth, social justice, love, and liberty. To suppress war or communism, which are only names and not realities, the causes of war and communism, which alone are realities, must be attacked. Pope John simply recognizes the old scholastic adage: "Take away the causes, and you take away the effect." With the causes eliminated by social justice, communism of necessity will have to change in the course of history. The professional anti-communist claims that this is impossible. These "thinkers," the Pope says, are not true students of history, for history shows that men and ideas change. If this is correct, then there is a chance and a hope for a true dialogue between Christianity and communism.[1] If not, the only alternative is to drop the bomb, which really solves nothing and, moreover holds imminent danger of destroying all. Nothing is solved, because the attempt to kill communism by thermonuclear war—besides being unchristian—would be unsuccessful, because ideas cannot be killed by bombs; it would succeed only in elimi-

---

[1] It is interesting to note that Paul VI has continued this same hope of dialogue in his most recent encyclical, *Ecclesiam Suam*. While openly condemning communism (as did, in fact, Pope John), Paul left the possibility of dialogue intact. If there is no dialogue, it cannot be attributed to any bad faith by the Church, but rather explained by the bad faith of the communists.

nating people while the essential vice, social injustice, would remain. The imminent danger of the insane annihilation of the human race is too real to need any commentary.

As the Pope saw it, man's only hope for peace is the program of *Mater et Magistra:* an all-out attack on the causes of inequality, social injustice, poverty, and human degradation, which attack alone is the order of peace. The only way to peace is a positive program of human betterment for all men and the opening possibility of dialogue. To shut off any possibility of dialogue by a sterile anti-communism is, in reality, to give up hope in God's grace and in human freedom. Such an attitude is basically inhuman and unchristian. In any case, the balance is always difficult to attain: the dangers and errors must be clear, but they must be condemned in such a way as not to exclude all possibility of fruitful dialogue, especially on those aspects which are positive and just on both sides. Pope John preferred to emphasize the latter, while Pius XII emphasized the former. This is not at all strange. What is important to emphasize at one time in pontifical teaching can receive lesser emphasis at another time. This shifting of emphasis is not the game of *real-politik*, but is the realization that human situations are continuously in evolution, even revolution, and that no two periods present quite the same circumstances in quite the same way.

III

The foundation stone of any just society is the degree to which it respects and promotes the rights of the human person, and in both *Mater et Magistra* and *Pacem in terris* this principle is clearly enunciated:

219. The fundamental principle in this doctrine

is that individual men are of necessity the foundation, the cause and the reason for the existence of all social institutions, insofar as men are social by nature and have been raised to the level of the supernatural realm. (*Mater et Magistra.*)

9. Any human society, if it is to be well ordered and productive, must lay down as a foundation this principle: that every human being is a person; his nature is endowed with intelligence and free will. By virtue of this, he has rights and duties of his own, flowing directly and simultaneously from his very nature, which are therefore universal, inviolable, and inalienable. (*Pacem in terris.*)

This principle is made the very touchstone of both of these momentous encyclicals of modern times. The Pope does not speak of all men in general, but of each individual man (*singulos homines*), and the whole of both letters shows clearly that the Pope is concerned with individual men and women, not with a nameless mass or a crowd. Society exists for the individual, not the individual for society. Thus, the tone of the whole two letters is personalistic, concerned with the protection and promotion of the human person. Yet, by nature, man is also a social being, and from that very fact, he bears a serious relation to other men. These two aspects, of course, lead to the paradox of who and what man is. The Pope attempts to balance these two equally demanding parts of man's nature: one can never be sacrificed for the other under any condition. The two extremes are carefully avoided by the Pope: the first, an exaggerated individualism which would over-emphasize individual traits and abilities and thereby gravely endanger man's necessary social relationship with his fellow man; and the second, an extreme collectivistic socialism in which the individual is absorbed into and is used for the total mission of the State.

By balancing the individual and the social demands of man's nature, the Church has evolved a whole body of social doctrine which is as authoritative as her very dogma.

> 220. From this bedrock principle, which safeguards and guarantees the sacred dignity of the individual, the Church has evolved, with the cooperation of enlightened priests and laymen, especially during the past century, a clear body of social doctrine. This doctrine points out the sure way to arrange men's social relations according to universal norms that conform with the nature of things, with the varying dimensions of contemporary society. Here, then, are norms which all men can accept.

There is grave danger in not understanding the proper basis of this "bedrock principle." As the Pope insists, the main objection to every totalitarian regime—and one that is really its death—is that, in such a conception, the social order is separated from God, the foundation of the dignity of man. While it is quite true that many men, who are not believers or who even reject any notion of a God, respect the deep dignity of man and endeavor with all of their energies to protect it,[2] there is grave danger in this attitude. The atheist or the non-believer is really caught in a dilemma. Either man has dignity issuing from a superior being and therefore

[2] Pope Paul VI admirably recognized this throughout his encyclical *Ecclesiam Suam.* He speaks very bluntly when he says that one of the causes of atheism today is Christians themselves. By not following the fundamental Christian precepts of love and justice, Christians have caused grave scandal to the modern world. Above all is this evidently true with regard the social teaching of the Church.

his person is inviolate, or man issues from the earth like the other animals around him. If the latter case were true, there could be no real argument with the communist or the totalitarian. Man's existence would simply be a case of "historic evolution" towards one or another political or ideological system or thought. Under what authority can the atheist call a halt to the manipulation of man in all of its modern forms: invasion of privacy, brain washing by propaganda and television media, status seeking and its pressures, materialism, euthanasia, and so on? Does man have a dignity above and beyond the animal, and, if so, does it make any sense to appeal to nature or reason for proof? Can such a man really attempt to stop or impede the slow disintegration of human rights? How and in what name is this sincere atheist to check such a trend? Theoretically, it is impossible for him to do so.

No matter how great the advance in science or technology, any particular society is in danger of corruption from within when it loses its religious roots. The order laid down by God will alone bring peace: "Peace on earth, which men of every era have so eagerly yearned for, can be firmly established only if the order laid down by God be dutifully observed" (*Pacem in terris,* par. 1). Man is not just a material phenomenon of nature; he is also a spiritul entity with rights and duties and, consequently, a dignity infinitely beyond that of any animal. It is noteworthy that in *Pacem in terris,* an encyclical dedicated to peace, so much emphasis is placed on the rights of man. The opening section directly mentions peace, but in the letter proper, the rights of man are more fully discussed than the idea of peace. This seeming disproportion is not illogical, for peace would be an empty mockery without the basic recognition of human rights. Peace is the fruit of justice, animated by a love of the objective order given by God. And justice demands above all else the acknowledgment that the human person is endowed with liberty, that is, with a natural right which bestows perfect equality on all men. Any advance in justice is therefore an advance of peace. Too many people confuse peace with an absence of war, with the maintenance of the *status quo*, with an abundance of material advantages. The foundation of peace, however, can only be justice animated by love, and the prime requisite of justice is that all men be regarded and respected as persons with inalienable rights and duties:

> 215. Wherefore, whatever the progress in technology and economic life, there can be neither justice nor peace in the world, so long as men fail to realize how great is their dignity; for they have been created by God and are His children. We speak of God, who must be regarded as the first and final cause of all things He has created. Separated from God, man becomes monstrous to himself and others. Consequently, mutual relationships between men absolutely require a right ordering of the human conscience in relation to God, the source of all truth, justice and love.

One of the important things in *Mater et Magistra* is the emphasis which the Pope gives to the necessity for teaching the Church's social doctrines at all levels, and thus for living this doctrine on all levels. The Pope speaks frankly when he says that it is a difficult task:

> 221. But it is indispensable, today more than ever, that this doctrine be known, assimilated and

translated into social reality in the form and manner which different situations allow or demand. Surely this is no easy task, but it is an exalted one. Our warm invitation to join in executing it goes out, not only to Our brothers and sons scattered throughout the world, but also to all men of good will.

To live the social teachings of the Church, a Christian must be prepared to suffer, and, most painful of all, he must be prepared to suffer at the hands of his fellow Christians. In his younger days when a professor at Rome, Pope John himself was on the carpet: he was reported to his Bishop by the Holy Office for taking the social ideas of Leo XIII too seriously in his teaching. He brings up the same point in *Pacem in terris:* because so much personal sacrifice is demanded, those who labor in this field are few, but he is confident that their number will grow.

164. Admittedly, those who are endeavoring to restore the relations of social life according to the criteria mentioned above, are not many; to them We express Our paternal appreciation, and We earnestly invite them to persevere in their work with ever greater zeal. And We are comforted by the hope that their number will increase, especially among Christian believers. For it is an imperative of duty; it is a requirement of love. Every believer in this world of ours must be a spark of light, a center of love, a vivifying leaven amidst his fellow men: and he will be this all the more perfectly the more closely he lives in communion with God in the intimacy of his own soul. (*Pacem in terris.*)

Yet the Pope insists that Christians work in the world. This insistence is shocking for those who would relegate the Church to the ivory tower of false spiritualism, tending to the things above with no concern for the realities of earth. This distorted piety is erroneous for two reasons. First, human action in any field is moral action and, by that very fact, must follow the moral principles which guide action in any human endeavor. If man's actions in the social, economic, and international fields are not the concern of the Church, it must be concluded that they are not moral endeavors, and such a conclusion is an absurdity. The Church would be derelict in her duty if she failed to enlighten her children on the underlying moral principles and basic moral demands in each of these particular fields. Second, an attitude of rejection by the Church of the economic and social sphere would be tantamount to a false spiritualism, a disincarnationalism, which has long tempted many Christians and Catholics within the Church. Dogma and social thought are not separate, but two sides of the same coin.

To preach a spiritual doctrine intact and free from error is the principal task of the Church through the hierarchy; but for this doctrine to effect salvation in the present world, however, it is imperative that the Church have the necessary and Christlike teaching authority to guide her children on the blood-and-guts problems of real life. Without this kind of teaching authority, the Church is radically impeded in exposing the mind of Christ on the agonizing problems that Christians are called upon to face each day. The Pope strongly opposes as erroneous the idea of a "spiritual" Christianity that is disengaged from the concrete affairs of men. His call for engagement is not a prefabrication of the

Church in a type of *real-politik,* but an extension of the gospel itself as applied to real men and women who live in space and time.

> 222. We reaffirm strongly that Christian social doctrine is an integral part of the Christian conception of life.
>
> Christianity is in a sense a joining together of earth with heaven in that it takes man concretely, spirit and matter, intellect and will, and bids him lift his mind up from the changing conditions in which men dwell together to the heights of heavenly life—where finally one will know the joy of unending happiness and peace.
>
> Hence, though Holy Church has the special task of sanctifying souls and making them partake of supernatural goods, she is also solicitous for the needs of men's daily life, not merely those having to do with bodily nourishment and the material side of life, but those also that concern prosperity and culture in all its many aspects and historical stages.

Man has a historical existence as well as a spiritual existence, and, from every point of view, his historical existence is in evolution. If the Church did not have the power to teach authoritatively on affairs of men as they evolve through history, she would be an a-historical religion that, like Buddhism or Hinduism, escapes from time and space. Whatever else may be said about these Eastern religions, they surely are not historical-incarnational religions; Christianity, on the contrary, lives or dies as it is injected into the veins of history and influences the minds of men. Take the incarnational reality from Christianity, and it is no longer Christianity.

The Church's social teaching is her life-line to the

modern world: without it, any form of *aggiornamento* becomes impossible, and Marx's accusation that religion is the opium of the people is verified. To keep the Church's incarnational reality pertinent to the modern world, the Pope strongly insists that its social teachings be promulgated at all levels, in all schools, by all means of communication:

> 223. On this account, We ardently desire that more and more attention be given to the study of this doctrine. While we note with satisfaction that in some schools it has been taught with success for years, We strongly urge that it be included as an item in the required curriculum in Catholic schools of every kind, particularly in seminaries. It is to be inserted into the religious instruction programs of parishes and of associations of the lay apostolate. It should be publicized by every modern means of mass communication—daily newspapers and periodicals, publications of both a scientific and a popular nature, radio and television.

In this needed effort, he makes a special appeal to laymen.

> 225. They should be convinced that the truth and efficacy of this teaching can most easily be demonstrated when they can show that it offers an effective solution for present-day difficulties. In this way they might bring it to the attention of those who oppose the doctrine through ignorance. Indeed, they may even cause a ray of its light to penetrate the minds of such men.

This teaching must be given most especially to laymen, and great efforts must be made to imbue them with its meaning and spirit. The reason is quite simple.

Above all others, laymen are the bridge between the Church and the modern world. They are not merely passive recipients and obedient robots; but, understanding that Christ has a message for the world through the social teaching of the Church, they must absorb it, adapt it, and give it practical implementation in their cultural and social surroundings.

226. It is not enough merely to publicize a social doctrine; it has to be translated into action. This is particularly true of Christian social doctrine, whose light is truth, whose objective is justice and whose driving force is love.

227. Hence it is most important not only that Our sons have an understanding of this social teaching, but that they be trained in it.

228. Christian education, if it is to be called complete, should concern itself with every kind of obligation. Hence it is essential that it should inspire the faithful to carry on their economic and social activities in accordance with the Church's teaching.

230. Consequently, for this type of education it is not enough that men be taught, in the light of the Church's doctrine, what their obligations as Christians are in the economic and social fields. They must also be given, through practical instruction, the means that will enable them properly to fulfill these duties.

The greatest evil that can happen to the Church is not persecution, for this can be and usually is salvific. Irrelevance is the greatest danger it can face. For the past four hundred years, the Church has tried to maintain its old habits of thought and life in circumstances which have made them increasingly ineffective. The influence of Christian thought on modern man has been slight, and the Christian faces the ugly fact that the world has developed and will continue to develop without him and sometimes in spite of him. "We do not fight the Church," said the Jacobins of the nineteenth century; "we simply bid it goodbye." The modern world might well agree. And, ironically, the Church has been sent to save and not to condemn the world. Through its social teaching the Church can be relevant to the modern world, which so sorely needs her spiritual guidance in constructing the city of man. As the Psalmist reminds us, "Unless the Lord builds the house, they labor in vain who build it." But the Church, through laymen, also has the grave obligation to understand modern man and his endeavors and to bring to bear the spiritual light of justice and charity on his complex problems. Because of the obligation's gravity, the Pope insists on the inculcation of this doctrine from the first days of the Catholic's education. Harboring no nostalgia for a defunct ecclesiastical medievalism, Pope John expresses the grandeur of modern man and points out how modern man can become even greater and more firm. His words are optimistic and positive, and they encourage Catholics to strive to further the ideals of modern man. Rededicating Catholic social thought, Pope John declares that it promotes individual civil rights and international rights, national integrity and UN solidarity. In other words, the approach of Pope John and that of his predecessors has been one of positive adaptation and accommodation to what is good in modern social and economic endeavors.

How is this Christian message to be made known to the people of the revolutionary twentieth century? To say that Christ and Christians are not interested in what is happening in the world is surely to relegate Christianity to a private pietistic affair of no consequence to modern man. Such a view is far from that of John XXIII. The neutral factor in this synthesis of Christ and the modern world is the layman who is imbued with the social teachings of the Church.

233. In social education, therefore, organizations of the lay apostolate must be accorded an important role, especially those that have as their purpose the Christianization of the economic and social sectors of the temporal order. For members of these associations can profit from their daily experiences in order to prepare themselves more thoroughly for this apostolate and then contribute to the formation of the younger generation.

240. From instruction and education one must pass to action. This is a task that belongs particularly to Our sons, the laity, since their work generally involves them in temporal activities and in the formation of institutions dealing with such affairs.

241. In performing such a noble task, it is essential that Our sons be professionally qualified and carry on their occupation in conformity with its own proper laws in order to secure effectively the desired ends. It is equally necessary, however, that they act within the framework of the principles and directives of Christian social teaching and in an attitude of loyal trust in filial obedience to ecclesiastical authority. Let them remember that when they fail to harmonize their activities with the social principles and directives taught by the Church and confirmed by Us, they fail in their obligations and often violate the rights of others. But they can even cast discredit on that very doc-

trine which appears as if it were noble enough in itself, but lacking in real power to control and regulate affairs.

The layman has a proper function in the Church. Consequently, his proper spirituality and sanctification must be sought in fulfilling his specific work: the incarnation of the divine life in the temporal domain.

If he is to bring out the image of God contained in the world, the layman must enter fully into all of the ramifications of the temporal order. In the true biblical sense of the word, the layman is God's lieutenant in creation, prolonging creation in accordance with the image of God and man given to him in faith. His proper mortification will be to purify continuously his own intentions, and not to despair when, at times, he sees no direct connection between his work and the Kingdom. If faith is demanded in God's mysteries—for man can never fully understand them—so too is faith required in restoring the temporal order to God, for man also does not fully understand all of its ramifications and consequences. But one thing must remain certain: in his research, in his laboratory, at his machine, at his microscope, in his struggle for just laws and social justice, the layman is doing God's will in prolonging creation and fulfilling his proper apostolate in the Church of God. In this sense, the layman partakes of the work of the Church in its full and cosmic sense. Taking encouragement from St. Paul, who originally had this gigantic and total vision of the Church and of Christ's triumph through it (Col. 1:15–20), a layman's proper vocation is to bring out Christ's image, to find it within things and consecrate himself to it. By virtue of creation, all is Christ's by right; the great dignity and ecclesial task of the layman is to make it His in fact, enabling Christ to reproduce His image, prolonging it through man's work in creation.

In short, the layman is to be incorporated into the living and dynamic body of the Church. The narrow and clerical concept of the Church which has persisted for a thousand years must be abandoned. It is necessary to return to a total view of a living Church and, above all, to a total view of the Church's task in the world, where everything has a religious though not necessarily supernatural meaning. Christians must again capture the total vision of the Church in its supernatural and natural commitment, consecrating the totality of the created order to Christ, who will only then be "all in all." For over five hundred years, Christianity has concentrated almost exclusively on the supernatural and neglected the ramifications and consequences of its dynamic doctrine on the practical lives of men. If religion, even the Christian religion, is separated from this longing and agony of modern men as men, then it is an opiate and an escape. Under such a separation of Church and man, the Christian might well be a Buddhist or a Neo-Platonist; under no circumstances can he be called a true Christian, at least if the gospel is taken seriously. Christianity, the most revolutionary dynamism which man has ever known, has atrophied into an innocuous fetish, a protection for the entrenched *status quo* of selfishness, and an escape from human compassion. A perfect case in point is Cuba and Latin America, where the Church has been swallowed by a specific cultural and intellectual milieu in which it is increasingly incapable of answering the revolutionary needs of the times. This is an example of what happens to the Church when it cannot correspond to the needs of contemporary men. It simply ceases to be a living force among men.

Though the theoretical concept of the layman's position in the Church has been established, yet what has been theoretically formulated has found no practical framework in which to function. Up to this point, lip service alone has been paid to the theological ideal. In the words of Bishop Lancaster Spalding, Catholics have not wanted to practice what they preach. Moreover, the present structure of canon law and the traditional parochial system in the United States have not permitted the Catholic to practice his preaching. Laymen have been invited to the Council, have been appointed to important positions on diocesan liturgical, architectural, and educational commissions, but these have been sporadic and far from the general rule. The clergy's fear of a totally defunct "lay-trusteeship" is all too prevalent, especially among the older bishops and clergy.

The younger clergy are somewhat more attuned to the needs of the day, but even they have received this education mostly "on the job" and not in the seminaries. The average diocesan seminary has made little or no progress in integrating the new concepts of lay theology into the traditional *Tractatus de Ecclesia*. Seminaries are doing a poor job of training priests for life in the world precisely because they are removed from any real contact with the world. This is indeed ironical, if not tragic. How is the young priest to be cognizant of the problems and thought of the layman when he is separated from them during his formative years? When the question of the virtues necessary for understanding the layman's position in the world arises, the unfortunate separation of seminarian and layman becomes particularly poignant. In seminary training, the virtues of obedience and docility are dominant. This emphasis is not in any way wrong, since the priesthood is essentially an auxiliary extension of episcopal power and jurisdiction. But these are not the virtues dominating the lives of laymen, where freedom, personal initiative, and creative thinking must constitute the heart and soul of any successful lay apostolate to and in the world.

Until practical measures for the broader participation of laymen in the life of the Church are specifically outlined, clerical-lay tensions will continue to grow. Because of their ill-defined role, many laymen see a sharp dichotomy between their properly "ecclesiastical" (sacral) functions and their lives as laymen. Pope John XXIII was right when he observed that the cause for this dichotomy "is to be found in an inconsistency in their minds between religious belief and their action in the temporal sphere. It is necessary, therefore, that their interior unity be re-established, and that in their temporal activity faith should be present as a beacon to give light, and charity as a force to give life" (*Pacem in terris*, par. 152). By the Church's failing to emphasize the total dynamic structure of the ecclesial community, the function of the layman with regard to his vocation in the created world has remained obscure. By not emphasizing incarnationalism, to use Chardin's term, perhaps the Catholic community has "sinned" by transcendence.

IV

Yet the Pope does not and cannot remain in the realm of theory. As a matter of fact, theory without action is once again disincarnationalism, an abandonment of the Church's task to other ideologies that are often foreign and hostile to the Christian spirit. To overcome this, the requirements for Christian social action must be practiced: learn the facts and understand the complex situa-

tion; judge this situation in the light of experience and
the Church's social teaching; and then form a plan for
concrete action:

> 236. In reducing social principles and directives
> to practice, one usually goes through three stages:
> reviewing the actual situation, judging it in the
> light of these principles and directives and decid-
> ing what can and what should be done to apply
> these traditional norms to the extent that the situa-
> tion will permit. These three stages are usually
> expressed in the three terms: observe, judge, act.

> 237. It is particularly important that young
> people should reflect often on this program and
> even more, as far as possible, follow it in practice,
> so that the doctrine they have learned will not be
> viewed merely as a set of abstract ideas but as
> something capable of being translated into deeds.

Thus education for action is the essential ingredient
for the fullness of Christian education, and, without this
kind of education, Christian doctrine remains sterile
and fruitless. Yet in the past, non-active pretty piety
characterized much of Christian education, where the
"world" (whatever that might be) was looked upon as a
place of temptation and sin and where the rules and
regulations were negatively based on "How far can I go
without sin?" This kind of education, of course, is a
caricature of the open and dynamic spirit of Christianity. Today Christian education must be receptive to the
values of the modern world and ready to engage it on its
own terms with optimism. The fearful distrust of the
modern world and its achievements is a thing of the
past.

In a sense, the Pope points out that a person can only
be formed by action. By applying Christian principles in

concrete situations, the Christian truly comes to know
what they mean. A man knows the poor only when he
works with and serves the poor and neglected; he
realizes the meaning of racial justice at a sit-in or in a
Mississippi county working for voting registration in the
midst of danger and hate; he knows the plight of the
economically underdeveloped nation only when he
works among them as a Papal Volunteer or a Peace
Corps worker. Doctrine and its theoretical inculcation is
an important essential for a proper orientation, but this
alone is simply not enough for the complete Christian.
He must bring that doctrine to a concrete situation and
make it into a living reality which incarnates the intention of Christ. This clear and emphatic statement on lay
action is in perfect keeping with Pope John's idea of the
aggiornamento, the Christian's confrontation of the
modern world. Action inspired by Christian social
thought can truly light the world. This idea runs
throughout the whole of *Mater et Magistra* and, in a
sense, sums up its spirit and intent.

In two remarkable paragraphs of the encyclical, Pope
John sums up what has been called Christian humanism
or the Christian meaning of temporal tasks:

> 255. Our Lord, in the course of His sublime
> prayer for the unity of the Church, made this
> request of the Father on behalf of His disciples: *I
> pray not that thou take them out of the world, but
> that thou keep them from evil.*
>
> We should not foolishly dream up an artificial
> opposition—where none really exists—between
> one's own spiritual perfection and one's active con-
> tact with the everyday world, as if a man could not
> perfect himself as a Christian except by putting
> aside all temporal activity, or as if, whenever he

engages in such activity, a man is inevitably led to compromise his personal dignity as a human being and as a believer.

256. Far from this being so, it is perfectly in keeping with the plan of Divine Providence that a man should develop and perfect himself through his daily work. And this work, for almost all human beings, is of a temporal nature.

Today, the Church is confronted with the immense task of giving a human and Christian tone to modern civilization. This is a labor that is urged on the Church and indeed is almost begged for by our age itself for the sake of its further development and even for its continued existence free from harm. As We have already emphasized, the Church turns for help in fulfilling this mission especially to her lay sons. They are thus committed to carry on their activities in such a way that they constitute the performance of a service done to others, but in intimate union with God, through Christ and for His greater glory.

St. Thomas also wrote some interesting pages in his *Summa Contra Gentes* on man's ability to share in the divine activity and causality of God. In these pages, St. Thomas revealed himself a true Christian humanist, for he affirmed that all created things somehow desire to be like their creator. This desire includes the imitation of God in His causality: man imitates this divine causality by discovering authentic values in the creation initially given to him. The Pope understands and extends this Christian theme to all men, whose vocations consist in directing, developing, or transforming the whole of the created world and its values. In the mind of the Pope, man's creative role is very small compared to the action and causality of the Provident Creator. Yet to the degree that men direct, develop, or transform creation according to the plan of the Creator, they are really collaborators of the Lord. And the Christian alone is properly equipped to effect this transformation and collaboration.

Non-believers, however, accuse the Christian of insincerity with regard to his work in the world. For the Christian, they argue, the temporal city of man is only a passing mirage of which he must make the best, but at the same time, he cannot take it seriously, for he awaits the Kingdom in another world. This charge of insincerity toward the temporal order is more to the point and more serious than the former accusations that religion is the opium of the people or that it is the propagator of social and class inequalities. Contemporary arguments maintain that religion is not only a detriment to social progress but is simply not pertinent to modern man and his world. And since religion and the Christian are irrelevant to modern man, there does not seem to be an intrinsic connection between Christ and the body temporal. Because the Christian lives for another world, the argument goes, he cannot take the temporal question seriously.

From the ranks of many spiritual writers, moreover, there seems to be a further confirmation of this same attitude. Perfection consists in detachment, they say, and the world is nothing but dust and vanity. In accomplishing his work in the temporal sphere, the Christian must have a pure intention in doing all for the love and service of God, even though these temporal actions have no ultimate value. All of man's activities have no direct relationship with heaven, since all is doomed to destruction. The only sure way of sanctifying human activity, argue these writers, is to offer all to God with the pure intention of love. Temporal activities are but mere occasions in which, moment by moment, man proves his love of God while on earth. In such a context, then, man's temporal vocation does not mean anything in itself insofar as the Kingdom is concerned; it has only an accidental value.

The objections posed by the non-believers and by these spiritual writers have this in common: each renders the temporal activity of the Christian insincere and useless. According to Father Teilhard de Chardin, three attitudes are possible for the Christian facing such a situation. The first is the monastic attitude of a total abandonment of the temporal world and its values. The second is a complete rejection of the Christian order and, consequently, a complete dedication to the temporal order. And the last is a refusal to attempt a rational reconciliation of Christianity with temporal functions, thereby escaping the problem. All three have one basic thing in common: they are all escapes from the original difficulty of discovering the relationship between the temporal and the Christian orders.

Moreover, there indeed are many examples in history of Christians refusing to take the temporal order seriously for its own sake. The Middle Ages, and St. Thomas Aquinas in particular, had already given a brilliant basis for a true Christian humanism. Unfortunately, from the time of the Middle Ages, no serious effort was made to incarnate these basic principles into the human realities of the city of man. The principles were there, but they were seldom taken seriously. Ironically enough, most of the accomplishments in the sociopolitical and temporal orders have been brought about either in opposition to the Church or by non-believers. And though many outstanding exceptions to this generalization could be cited, nonetheless it remains quite accurate. When presented with each of the temporal revolutions in thought and action, the general attitude of the Christian community and its leaders was clear: one of opposition and harassment.

For example, elements of social doctrine in the early and late nineteenth century were worked out by non-Catholics who developed a consciousness of social needs. It comes as somewhat of a shock to learn that the first man in the history of modern times to develop a full and complete philosophy of work as a true human value, worthy in itself and not to be sold as a commodity, was a materialistic atheist, Karl Marx. Christianity already had in its tradition all of the basic principles for the development of such a philosophy and theology; nevertheless, this development did not take place systematically before Marx. Even when Leo XIII wrote his encyclical *Rerum Novarum* in 1891, many Catholics refused to accept his social teaching. This refusal was indeed indicative that the temporal order was not taken seriously by most Christians. Until recent years, moreover, the name of Sigmund Freud was an anathema in most Catholic circles. That most Catholics refused to examine his empirical findings apart from his philosophic prejudices was still another evident sign of the Catholic refusal to take research, technology, and the psychic sciences seriously. Catholics have long been reminded, both here and abroad, that in spite of the Church's vast expenditures in the field of education, no Catholic Oppenheimer, Einstein, or Freud has appeared.

Outside of certain pontifical documents, there has been little effort on the part of Catholics to formulate a body of systematic thought on international government and organization. The Catholic, more than anyone else, should lead in creating world unity because he firmly understands the meaning of one humanity created and redeemed by God. It is indeed noteworthy that the U.N. was conceived and brought about by non-Catholics, and, if anything, American Catholics at least are noted for their opposition to such movements. And, finally, what can be said about the Catholic attitude toward the social evolution in the notions of slavery, feminism, and the penal law? For centuries, human bondage, female inequality, and cruelties in law were allowed to exist in the bosom of the Church with little or no effort to better them. Since these evils were basically social, they could be remedied only by a reform of social thought on these questions; it was a work of the temporal order that had to be brought about in that order. Certainly, all the principles necessary for such an evolution existed in Christianity: the doctrine of the equality of and differences between man and woman, the notion that in Christ there is neither "slave or free man," and the concept of Christian mercy and forgiveness tempering justice in law. All this existed as in seed in the corpus of Christian doctrine, but its implantation, its incarnation into temporal institutions could only come about by taking the temporal order seriously and by attempting to humanize and Christianize it by positive action. In all sincerity, the Catholic has not applied himself in the world since the time of the Middle Ages. This had resulted in the non-believer's indictment: "The Christian is incapable of transforming the temporal order because he cannot take it seriously." From what has been said, it would seem that this charge is all too true.

The Christian, however, feels most uneasy with this accusation. Faced with the vast and ever-expanding world of technology and culture, he wants to understand his modern condition with reference to his faith. He wants to question his faith to see whether it can give him an answer to the sometimes agonizing problems of modern living. He seeks to know, in short, what Christ thinks of his world, his modern world, his creations, and, consequently, he seeks to know Christ's judgment. Is it true, he asks, that the temporal has no value, no intrinsic meaning for the Christian? Can he really participate in the temporal with all of its ramification only halfheartedly—or, what would be yet worse, must he have no real sincerity toward terrestrial things? Is there any intrinsic connection between his temporal vocation and the Kingdom of Christ? These are serious questions for at least two reasons. First, if the temporal order as such has no value, it means the idea that the universe is God's creation and that man participates and continues this initial act of creation through his work is without value. Second, if the temporal has no value as such for eternity, then it must follow that the modern world and modern man must remain forever strangers to Christ and Christianity. If the values of the modern world are not recognized as legitimate values for Christianity, in the long run they mean nothing at all.

The first reason borders on blasphemy. It means that the Christian has no genuine interest in, or fundamental interpretation of, what God initially created and continuously keeps in being. In order to claim that God's creation and man's work upon it is destined for total destruction, many of the texts of the New Testament must be ignored or misread. The second position, on the other hand, is an indirect denial of the catholicity and universality of the Church, since she adapts herself to all cultures and races. To compare these cultures to a cloak which Christianity puts on and takes off at diverse times in her history runs counter to the deepest aspirations of man. In its final form, this attitude means that almost all of man's activities have, in the long run, no real meaning for eternal life or God.

Human realities of whatever order can have a religious, even though not a sacred, meaning. Every creature, including man's creations in art, society, technology, science, music, sculpture, trade and so on, is in its final root good. For the Christian and the Bible, all creation is good in its origin in God and in its development through man, who is God's "image and likeness." The applications of this principle will have an important bearing on the Christian interpretation of the temporal. Moreover, all types of Catholic literature dealing with the Catholic layman have stressed that the temporal order is his proper domain. Indeed, theologians have made a number of vigorous attempts to integrate the layman's temporal vocation within the Kingdom of Christ. Since the temporal is the layman's proper domain, the crux of the problem has been to give the temporal a profound Christian signification. With such a vision of faith, the layman must enter the field of human values fully, completely, and without reserve.

If these observations are correct, the layman's temporal activities *can* have a religious, even if not a properly sacred, meaning. The word *can* is purposely stressed because culture and technology are often ambiguous. Their fundamental orientations are good, but they can be used for evil by evil men. It is presupposed that the intention of the Christian will always be purified and good. But even beyond this, true technological and cultural progress has, we believe, a meaning intrinsic to itself; and, therefore, the possibility for its eventual good use exist in its very root. Furthermore, the layman should not enter these fields from any apologetic prompting. His purpose is not to defend the faith (though this is not excluded), but to bring out the image of God in each of the temporal realities in which he engages. As Cardinal Mercier remarked: "We must form men, and many of them, who will devote themselves to science for its own sake, without any professional aim, without any apologetic intentions; men who will work at first hand to fashion the material needed for the edifice of science and thus contribute to its progressive construction." And again: "It is important to search in an unprejudiced way for the truth, the whole truth, without being in the least preoccupied with the consequences."

Is it not possible to see a certain spiritualization involved in establishing harmony in the material order? Can we not see in the struggle against suffering and death an attempt by man, even now on earth, to realize in part the glorious Kingdom of Christ, where there will be "neither suffering nor groan nor tear"? Can we not see in science an attempt to rationalize matter, to bring man closer to that intricate harmony with nature which was originally intended by God before the fall, and which will be fully accomplished in the glorious world to come? Even in the psychological sciences, can we not see an attempt to integrate man with himself and his brothers, preparing him for a true oblative love after being freed from morbid states of self-love and egocentrism?

V

It has justly been said that the Church's social teachings are nothing more than the application of the original brotherhood of men in a creation where justice and harmony reigned supreme. By the Redemption, this brotherhood was elevated to a more sublime height, but not radically changed. Furthermore, the elements of justice are presupposed in any true existence of charity, and justice has been accurately defined as the minimal demand for the existence of charity. Pius XI said that one must feed a man before one can speak of God to him: analogously, this is what the layman attempts to do by changing and inspiring the temporal structures of society. The whole domain of the body politic and the people temporal is his area of work. The layman, therefore, will have ample occasion to prepare for superior revelation by plunging unreservedly into all of the ramifications of the human social spheres. The notions of capital punishment, insurance and social security for the aged, evolving educational structures in a rapidly changing society, rehabilitation laws and services to prepare men for the technological age, responsible welfare programs guarding both justice and personal dignity, humanization of penal laws through co-operation among social scientists, psychologists, clergy, and jurists —these are a few examples of the tremendous responsibilities which await the layman in this temporal role. Catholic participation is also needed in medical and scientific research on disease, in space exploration for man's welfare, in the production of food for ever-growing populations, and in the industrialization of whole continents. There is a need for more demographic studies in immigration and over-population, for fresh efforts in housing, construction and urban renewal, and for continued thought on sociological problems.

After the encyclical *Mater et Magistra*, it would almost seem superfluous to mention the need for Catholic work and co-operation in international organizations for peace and harmony among nations. Aid to underdeveloped countries is most essential so that they may gain that minimum of self-respect needed for *human* society. Many such organizations have already come to birth in order to minister to these needs: WHO, UNESCO, MEDICO, Aid, the Grail, the Peace Corps and many other groups, both Catholic and non-sectarian.

If it is not to be impoverished by a narrow "supernaturalism," the total Christian order must include novelists, poets, painters, sculptors, composers, playwrights, and quality productions in television and the cinema. In its proper domain, each of the creative arts will reflect the true image of man in all his contradiction, agony, weakness, and glory. Christians must become leaders in these fields. If this work is left to the materialist, the pragmatist, or the communist, the result will only be a caricature of man's true image. Men such as Graham Greene, Bernanos, Marcel, Mauriac, Dolly, Van Gogh, and Beethoven have contributed greatly to this Christian vision of man's values in relation to the Kingdom.

These fields and many others are ripe for the harvest, the reception of the spiritual orientation of the modern world and modern man. Laymen must, as it were, plunge into this task with all its agonies, with all the difficulties it is bound to produce. The layman's thinking of what his position in the Church means for his proper spirituality will have to undergo an almost complete metamorphosis. And this proper spirituality will be based squarely on the knowledge that the layman is Christ's testimony, that he is Christ's and God's prolongation in the temporal order, developing and seizing it in all its riches. The layman's work in itself will then be the image of God and an expression of the dignity of man, both serving to glorify God and to sanctify man.

It will not be easy for the layman to change his usual notions of spirituality. Traditionally, the layman has been thought of as a priest or a religious in miniature. Though he could not go "all the way," he should go as

far as he could in his "state of life." Like the religious
and the priest, his mentality was geared more to the
sacral, to the specifically supernatural elements in life,
and the things of the "world" were to be used carefully
and cautiously. What really mattered, the all in all, was
the supernatural, the sacraments, and the Church—the
Church conceived, not in its cosmic dimensions, but
in its narrower hierarchic sense of closed liturgical
worship. Though the essentials which are common to all
Catholics—the sacraments, the Holy Sacrifice, and the
teaching authority of the Church—will always remain
unchanged because they are men's nourishment as Sons
of God, yet the other half of sanctity—the Apostolate—
is also necessary if the supernatural reality is to be made
flesh in the vision of man. Christian holiness or sanctity
is thus composed of two essential traits: the divine life
communicated in the Church through the sacraments,
and an apostolate that extends or incarnates this divine
reality. At times, the incarnational task will be extremely painful and agonizing. The layman will not
always feel a tangible "spiritual" result, as when he
makes a novena or says a rosary or goes to a Communion
breakfast or even raises money for the Church. But the
difficulty of the task will temper the Catholic's commitment to Christ and man.

The Pope ends his encyclical with a specific appeal to
Catholics in what constitutes the very core of their lives
and reality: the Mystical Body of Christ.

> 258. And so We cannot conclude Our encyclical,
> Venerable brothers, without recalling that most
> sublime and true tenet of Catholic doctrine which
> teaches us that we are living members of the Mysti-
> cal Body of Christ, which is the Church: *For as the
> body is one and has many members; and all the*

members of the body, many as they are, from one body: so also is it with Christ.

259. For this reason We strongly urge Our children everywhere, both clerical and lay, to remain thoroughly conscious of the extent of their dignity and high rank. These, in fact, are based on their oneness with Christ as branches with a vine: *I am the vine, you are the branches,* and on their ability to share in His divine life.

Hence, when Christians put themselves to work —even if it be in a task of a temporal nature—in conscious union with the divine Redeemer, every effort becomes a continuation of the effort of Jesus Christ and is penetrated with redemptive power: *He who abides in me, and I in him, he bears much fruit.* It thus becomes a more exalted and more noble labor, one which contributes to a man's personal spiritual perfection, helps to reach out and impart to others on all sides the fruits of Christian redemption. It further follows that the Christian message leavens, as it were, with the ferment of the Gospel the civilization in which one lives and works.

In reality, the layman's or the priest's vocation is a more secondary consideration in the Christian dispensation. The Catholic's fundamental vocation is to become a Christ, a vocation which each Catholic received at baptism and confirmation. Through these sacraments, Catholics forever belong to Christ and, in Him, to each other in a deeply mysterious social relationship that is called the Mystical Body of Christ. In this relationship, men are joined in real bonds of love and life so intimately and closely that earthly comparison is totally incapable of expressing it. In the Mystical Body, men are truly brothers and sisters in Jesus Christ, the Lord. This realization—which is often lightly felt among Christians—can give an impetus and a dynamism to all human endeavors in the social order. Man's thirst for justice can thus find its living water in the well-spring of charity and love in Christ. Catholics ought to strive to incarnate these ideals into the reality of the world. Painful and discouraging as it may often become to accomplish, the goal of the earthly city must be to reflect in some degree that which will be perfect only in the celestial city: perfect justice, perfect liberty, perfect truth and, above all, perfect love. As the same beloved Pontiff stated in *Pacem in terris,*

> 36. Human society, Venerable Brothers and beloved children, ought to be regarded above all as a spiritual reality: in which men communicate knowledge to each other in the light of truth; in which they can enjoy their rights and fulfill their duties, and are inspired to strive for moral good. Society should enable men to share in and enjoy every legitimate expression of beauty, and encourage them constantly to pass on to others all that is best in themselves, while they strive to make their own the spiritual achievements of others. These are the spiritual values which continually give life and basic orientation to cultural expressions, economic and social institutions, political movements and forms, laws, and all other structures by which society is outwardly established and constantly developed.

This passage is reminiscent of a passage of the Apocalypse:

> I saw the Holy City, the new Jerusalem, coming down out of heaven, prepared as a bride adorned

for her husband; and I heard a great voice from the throne saying, "Behold, the dwelling of God is with men. He will dwell with them, and they shall be His people."

(Apoc. 21:2–3.)

Index I

Rather than give a detailed analysis of the text of *Mater et Magistra,* we thought it more profitable to list the major subject headings with their corresponding paragraphs. We have also given the corresponding references from *Pacem in Terris* for reasons of comparison of the two encyclicals.

	Mater et Magistra	*Pacem in terris*
Agriculture:	84–85, 124–152	
Balance:	48, 54, 69, 73, 78, 80–81, 125, 127, 135, 136, 148, 157, 160, 165, 185–186, 192	37, 65, 72
Charity:	6, 38, 39, 43, 120, 158, 226, 257	35, 37, 45, 107, 129, 146, 163, 167, 177
Church:	1, 3, 11, 16, 25, 39, 42, 180, 184, 195, 208, 217, 249, 262	14, 160
Colonialism:	49, 172	42–43
Common good:	20, 21, 27, 40, 44, 52, 55, 65, 71–72, 78, 80, 96, 117, 140–141, 147, 151, 174	7, 25–26, 46, 48, 53, 55–57, 70, 84–85, 124, 132–139, 155
Communism:	23, 34	158–159
Contract:	18, 31–32, 75, 77, 84	
Co-operatives:	85, 87, 146, 163	101
Dignity:	1, 18, 71, 83, 111, 179, 190–191, 215, 220, 242–243, 259	9–10, 14, 20–21, 34, 38, 44, 73, 79, 86, 89, 122, 144
Disarmament:	69, 198, 203–204	109–119, 126–129

Index I

	Mater et Magistra	Pacem in terris
Economy:	11–14, 23, 34, 37–38, 40, 42, 37–74, 104, 164, 168, 173, 175	11, 18, 130–131
Education:	195, 197, 224, 227, 229, 230–232	13, 17, 153
Emigration:	45, 153–155	25, 102, 107–108
Enterprise:	20, 32, 35, 75, 77, 83, 91–93, 104, 142, 245	
Family:	43, 45, 55, 112, 144, 157, 193, 250	15–16, 19, 64, 106, 130, 164
Hierarchy of Values:	52, 106–107, 175–176, 234, 243–245, 257	57, 150
Initiative:	22, 51, 55, 57, 62, 65, 109, 120, 141, 151, 162, 148, 203	18, 23, 34, 65–66
Intermediary Bodies:	37, 52, 59, 65, 147	24, 64, 72, 130, 140, 164
Justice:	18, 33, 43, 59–68, 69–73, 78, 83, 94, 103, 110, 112, 122, 128–130, 150, 157–160, 205, 215, 226, 257, 261	20–21, 27, 35, 45, 53, 69, 91, 95–97, 112, 114, 144, 149, 154, 161–163, 167, 171
Layman:	220, 224, 231, 233, 240–241, 254, 256, 258–259	157, 161
Liberty:	31, 45, 55, 63, 109–110, 193–195, 232	24, 35, 37, 40, 45, 120, 124, 149, 155, 167
Marriage:	193–195	15–16
Over-population:	188–192, 196–202	
Person:	18, 21, 55, 62, 74, 91, 106–107, 125, 142, 149, 157, 209, 211, 220–221, 249, 255–256	9–18, 20, 24, 26, 28, 34, 41, 44, 47, 65, 73, 79, 139, 144, 158
Progress:	47–48, 54, 59–60, 73–74, 79–87, 106–107, 128–130, 168, 173, 181–182, 184, 200–201, 209–211, 243, 245–247	2–3

INDEX I

	Mater et Magistra	*Pacem in terris*
Property *(private)*:	18, 30, 32, 35, 37, 43, 45, 61, 74–75, 77, 84, 91–93, 105–107, 109, 111–115, 118–120	21–22
Responsibility:	9, 48, 55, 62–63, 82–84, 90–91, 99, 112, 118, 174, 176–177, 195, 203, 241, 253, 256	13, 23, 25, 28–30, 34–35, 44, 64, 86–87, 91–92, 120
Salary:	18, 31, 33, 70–71, 73, 75, 77, 79, 81–82, 107, 110, 115, 138, 150, 152, 168, 173	11, 20
Self- *Financing:*	75, 77	
Socialism:	34, 110	
Socialization:	59, 60–68, 105–109	65
Social *Security:*	48, 59, 60–61, 105–106, 135–136	11, 64, 156
Social *Teaching:*	4, 6, 9, 15, 25, 37, 50, 52–54, 71–72, 83–85, 111, 122–123, 126, 142, 208, 219–221, 226–230, 233–234, 236, 238, 245, 249, 254, 261	153, 157
State (role of):	11, 20–21, 44, 49, 52–54, 56, 62, 64–66, 71, 79, 99, 104, 116–118, 120, 124–145, 150, 160–161, 165	42, 46–50, 52, 64–65
Subsidiarity *(principle of):*	52–53, 117	26, 66, 140–141
Underdeveloped *Countries:*	48, 150–177	88, 101–102, 109, 121–125
Unemployment:	13, 48, 54, 71	11, 64
Unions:	11, 22–23, 25, 48, 91–93, 96–97, 99–103, 143–144	64, 156

Index I

	Mater et Magistra	*Pacem in terris*
Work:	18, 33, 42, 44, 55, 61, 71, 82–83, 92, 107, 112, 125, 149–150, 250, 256	18
Workers:	22–23, 25, 32, 68, 75, 77, 82–84, 91–96, 115, 125, 146, 149	20, 40, 102

Index II

The following are the diverse chapters of *Mater et Magistra* and the page where they can be found in this book.

M & M		M & M	
	Page		*Page*
18.	111–112	84.	56
20.	7	85.	133
22.	29, 36–37	89.	133
32.	48–50	91.	51, 99
34.	2, 13	92.	51–52, 94, 99
36.	23, 229	93.	54
37.	10	97.	37, 47–48, 100
43.	65–66	98.	100
47.	14	99.	26–27
48.	14–15, 47, 54	100.	29, 30
49.	15	101.	29, 30
50.	XI	102.	29, 30, 55
51.	8	103.	29, 30
53.	8, 98	104.	97–98
54.	169–170	105.	69–70
56.	11–12	106.	70, 110
57.	12	107.	70, 110
58.	12	109.	81
60.	18	110.	83–84
61.	19	111.	80
62.	20, 39–40	113.	96
63.	39–40	114.	96
64.	21, 39–40	115.	88–89, 99
65.	10, 25	116.	9–10, 82–83
66.	10, 12	117.	10, 93, 98
67.	22	118.	89
73.	118–119	124.	134–135
75.	48	127.	135
76.	49	128.	119
77.	49, 170	129.	136
80.	170–171	132.	137
82.	55	133.	137
83.	55–56, 112	136.	72, 137

Index II

M & M

	Page
137.	130
138.	130
142.	123, 138–139
143.	139
144.	138
145.	140
146.	36, 41, 126–127
149.	140–141
151.	11
152.	10–11
155.	145
156.	145–146
157.	143–144
158.	144, 186
159.	186–187
161.	147
162.	148
163.	149–150
165.	152, 187–188
171.	154
172.	154
173.	154
175.	57, 189
176.	189
187.	157
188.	157–158, 164
189.	158
190.	158–159, 164
191.	165
192.	165–166
195.	160
196.	162

M & M

	Page
197.	162
200.	166
201.	166–167
202.	167
203.	155–156
204.	156
213.	196
215.	194, 203
216.	195
217.	194–195
219.	199–200
220.	201
221.	203–204
222.	5, 206
223.	207
225.	207
226.	208
227.	208
228.	208
229.	108
230.	208
233.	210
236.	215
237.	215
238.	2
240.	210
241.	210
255.	216
256.	217
257.	114
258.	227–228
259.	xii, 112–113, 228

The following are the diverse chapters of *Pacem in terris* and the page where they can be found in this book.

Pacem

	Page
1.	202
9.	105, 200
11.	27, 60, 73, 79, 106
12.	19, 28
13.	28, 60
18.	18, 106
19.	19, 67–68
20.	19, 79
21.	66–67
22.	67
26.	27, 54
27.	54

Pacem

	Page
54.	89, 104
55.	104
56.	104
64.	36
65.	9
66.	9
98.	191
117.	84–85
152.	214
159.	196–197
164.	164

Index III

American Hospital Assoc., 76
Alliance for Progress, 105, 176
Anti-Poverty Bill (1964), 109, 147
Aswan Dam, 166
Bagdikan, B. H., 178
Barth, K., 91
Beethoven, L. van, 226
Bernanos, G., 226
Blue Cross, 74
Blue Shield, 74
Buddhism, 206
Carrasco, R. V., 173
Catholic Charities, 21
Chardin, Pierre Teilhard de, 192, 214, 219
Civil Rights Bill (1964), 46, 69, 80
Closed Shop, 38
Coffin, F. M., 148
Cort, J. C., 94
Discrimination, 178–180
Disincarnationalism, 205
Dolly, S., 226
Einstein, A., 220
E. P. T. A. 63
F. A. O., 144, 147
Franco, F. 29
Freud, S., 220
Galbraith, K., 127
Gibbons, Cardinal, 31
Goldwater, B., 34
Gompers, S., 32
Grail, 226
Greene, G., 226
Gremillion, J. B., 65
Häring, B., 162

Harrington, M., 77, 178–79
Haubtman, P., 79
Higgins, G. C., 29
Hilary, St., ix
Hinduism, 206
Hyde, D., 117
I. L. O., 30–31, 58–63
Janssens, L., 101
Jewish Relief Fund, 21
Katzenstein, R., 172
Kennedy, J. F., 154, 174
Keyserling, L., 181
Khrushchev, N., 197
Knights of Labor, 31
Labor Leader, 46
Latifundias, 89, 117
Leclercq, J., 102
Lenin, 29
Leo XIII, 6–7, 31–32, 111, 204, 220
Liberalism, Economic, 56, 68, 69, 90
Lichter, S., 70
Lucey, R. E., Archbishop, 46, 125
Marcel, G., 226
Maritain, J., 192
Masse, B., 73
Mauriac, F., 226
Marx, 5, 54, 109, 161, 207, 220
Marxism, 2–3, 32, 56, 85, 173
May, E., 22
McCormack, A., 147
McLoin, G., 171
Medicare, 21, 62, 73–75
M.E.D.I.C.O., 226
Mussolini, B., 29

Myrdal, G., 182
Mystical Body of Christ, xiii, 111, 115, 187, 227
N.A.M., 42
Nazism, 29
Neo-Platonism, 212
Nevins, A., 175
Nigeria, 119–122
N.L.R.B., 38, 41
Nuclear Weapons, 193
O'Brien, H. J., Archbishop, 38
Open Shop, 42
Oppenheimer, 220
Papal Volunteers, 188, 216
Paul VI, 91, 165, 168, 198
Peace Corps, 188, 216
Pius XI, 9, 13, 98, 107, 111, 225
Pius XII, x, 6, 17, 27, 32, 66, 79, 93, 96, 110–111, 192
Planning, xi
Political Democracy, 54–59
Quadragesimo Anno, 9, 22, 48, 96, 106
Rural Development Program, 131
Rerum Novarum, x, 24, 106, 220

Riga, P., 13, 71
Right to Work Laws, 33–40
Right Wing, 42
Rummel, J. R., Archbishop, 45–46
Scheyven, R., 146
Social Democracy, 54–59
Spalding, L., Bishop, 204
St. Thomas, 67, 102, 217, 219
Taft-Hartley Act (1947), 38
Tax Cut Bill (1964), 136–137, 182
Terrestial Realities, 4, 222
Tennessee Valley Authority, 83, 87
United Nations, 145, 168, 209
U.N.E.S.C.O., 226
Union Shop, 38
Universal Declaration of the Rights of Man, 59–60
Van Gogh, 226
Vatican Council II, 193
Villain, J., 116
Vizzard, J. F., 122
Ward, B., 150
Wetbacks, 124–125, 178
W.H.O., 226
World Council of Churches, 21
Zimmerman, A., 160